Ideas and intervention

Also by Joe Bailey

Social theory for planning

Ideas and intervention

Social theory for practice

Joe Bailey

Routledge & Kegan Paul
London, Boston and Henley

First published in 1980
by Routledge & Kegan Paul Ltd
39 Store Street, London WC1E 7DD,
Broadway House, Newtown Road,
Henley-on-Thames, Oxon RG9 1EN and
9 Park Street, Boston, Mass. 02108, USA
Set in Times by Computacomp (UK) Ltd
Fort William, Scotland
and printed in Great Britain by
Lowe & Brydone Ltd Thetford, Norfolk

British Library Cataloguing in Publication Data

Bailey, Joe

Ideas and intervention.
1. Sociology
I. Title
301'.01   HM24   79–42875

ISBN 0 7100 0367 6
ISBN 0 7100 0459 1 Pbk

Contents

Preface and acknowledgments

Sociology, more than most disciplines, is unstable. A concern with theory has ebbed and flowed a number of times in its history and we appear to be about to enter another period of impatience with theorizing as a reaction to the last decade's avid abstractionism. This book is an attempt to describe the relevance of theorizing against such a mobile and fraught background. In particular the recent tendency of theorizing to self-generation and of theorists to be seduced away from the objects of theory (other people's concerns or a 'primitive' perception of social problems) forms the immediate academic context.

This book is a response to some of the problems I have encountered in teaching 'sociological theory' to students in sociology departments and in a variety of vocational areas. There is a closure in theory which is potentially hermetic. This is often dealt with by the theorist by, in effect, abandoning sociology as a discipline concerned with problems suffered by people and implicitly advocating theory itself as a way of avoiding these problems by redefining them into purely abstract terms. This is not enough. There are no purely philosophical solutions, and students generally sense this and often reject theory (and sometimes sociology with it) as a result.

But theory is relevant because it is unavoidable.

I would like to thank the Organization of Sociologists in Polytechnics for permission to include in chapter 6 part of a previously published paper.

This book is for Caro, Anna and Josh.

1 Sociology's place

Sociology is not enjoyed, used or approved yet sociology is taught as a formal discipline to increasing numbers of people. This is a paradox. Sociology has until recently in its, so far brief, institutional life existed in an atmosphere of internal disagreement and external uncertainty. Sociology now suffers internal schism and external hostility. This is a crisis. The paradox and the crisis make the present time for sociology something of a climacteric. Put plainly, I fear that the potential good in sociology will be destroyed as its institutional existence becomes increasingly questioned. This questioning is only partly justified, but it is responding to the dogmatism, feebleness, amorality and arrogance that flowers in so much of sociology now. The recent proliferation of sociological sects is healthy and interesting but the abandonment in the process of all common, broad goals with respect to activism, teaching, scholarship and research is the beginning of a holy war of attrition.

It was not always so. The history of British sociology suggests that while there have been problems surrounding its institutionalization, especially up to the First World War, the internecine strife which existed in the nascent discipline was always within a very broad framework of agreed intentions. The general tradition within which such apparently opposed approaches as administrative data-gathering, ameliorism and social evolutionism competed for supremacy was one of interventionism.[1] The external circumstances were threatening even then. As Abrams makes clear, the role of 'sociologist' remained only a potential for a very long time and in great part this was due to institutional resistances over which such potential sociologists had no control. Then as now. But then internal

1

dispute resulted in the peaceful co-existence of different sociologies. Such pluralism and tolerance could be said to be in great part one of the reasons for the existence of sociology as a discipline. This is not to praise the quality of the newly born subject, or to deny that a different mix of approaches (civics, eugenics, Boothism, etc.) would not have improved the quality of present-day sociology. It is simply to say that if the establishment of sociology had waited upon a contest to be won, certain styles and theoretical traditions to be vanquished and somehow extinguished, we would be waiting yet. If such a pluralism was important in the conception, why has it become so redundant in the subsequent nurturing? Why can progress now be talked about only in terms of the destruction of obstacles (for instance the getting rid of 'residual' functionalism) and the ascendency of one particular approach (for instance historical materialism)?

This all sounds like complaining for its own sake. One of the aims of this book is to evaluate a purely critical sociology and to suggest that sociology can and should be constructive. Following my own advice, I ask what do I want sociology to be?

Most importantly I want sociology to be a servant and not a master, a means and not an end. But to what end? Barrington Moore has tried to discuss the universal, institutional conditions of human misery and unhappiness in a way that social scientists, parochial as they are, have completely neglected.[2] By extension one can ascribe to sociology the task of reducing misery. This is one bald and unexceptionable programme for justifying all organized intellectual activity. At this stage one need not be more explicit than this. Even by such an apparently idealistic and general prospectus a great deal of contemporary sociology, even where it claims to 'demystify', appears self-indulgent and inward-looking. In order to reduce misery, promote happiness and in some way deal with the problems of men and women sociology must have an institutional existence. Great intellectuals have often avoided universities like the plague (for instance Condorcet, Goethe, Marx), yet their own thought was nurtured by, created in opposition to, or founded upon, bodies of knowledge intimately connected with university-based scholarship.

Sociology is a discipline which has a benevolent potential

which will die if the discipline now becomes institutionally weak, for it cannot survive outside of institutions of higher education. The ideological and institutional weight of sociology are intimately connected. In this, I think, Gouldner is right when he highlights the importance of the social organization of sociological theory.[3] Organization must mediate between theory and practice, though whether the need is for a Lenin rather than a more pluralist figure I am doubtful.[4] Gouldner's call for the formation of theoretical collectives to re-establish the conditions of rational discourse is élitist and, more significantly, unnecessary if the members of the discipline could understand their own place between ideology and institution.

Who is being addressed here? Sociology cannot change under its own steam. It can never make itself accepted, and therefore the audience cannot be restricted to sociologists themselves. The audience is all those who use sociology and who ask sociology questions. Such audiences range from policy-makers at various levels and of various types, to collective interests, to practical social workers (conceived broadly), to students of sociology. No particular use is being prescribed here at this stage, merely the fact of use. It is true that sociology can simply be experienced as, for instance, liberation, intellectual growth or increased authenticity. Many students of sociology demand this sort of individual satisfaction from the discipline and from their teachers. This is very valuable and important when it happens, though I am sceptical of the possibility of a discipline such as sociology, which has little aesthetic or poetic profundity,[5] delivering the goods. It does happen, but almost by chance, and the experience of personal growth or transcendence which sociology sometimes provides is parasitical upon its ability to be used by others than sociologists.

Historically sociology has addressed its users.[6] The pursuit of sociological knowledge by thought and by action (and then by thought again), even the most apparently scholastic, has a practical end. It often seems that improving one's preaching to the already converted has been the goal, but this is really something of an exaggeration based on the fact that scholars talk to one another before talking to potential users. All seekers after truth believe that the truth will set us free. However, the concern with wider audiences characteristic of the growth of sociology has recently decayed. This may be due in part simply to the growth of institutional sociology whereby the actual numbers of inward-looking purists has increased.[7] The dramatic fact appears to be that more and more time is spent in arguing with ourselves.[8]

This book is addressed to sociologists and all those who think that there might be some use in sociology. It suggests that sociology can be rescued from the clutches of contemporary sociologists, who think they are philosophers or warriors, and given a genuine job of enlightenment. It proposes a calculation of the relations between theory and practice, between special kinds of thinking which have come to be called sociological theory and particular kinds of social practice which we might call, loosely, 'intervention'. It proposes this in a modest sense. No overall theoretical scheme is described which will provide the panacea for sociology's intellectual ills and the key to new liberating action. The case is made only that self-conscious calculation is better than blind and deaf assumption. The more we think about our action the better that action will be. Certainly this must be the root of rational activity itself rather than just of optimism. Yet what we might loosely call 'interventionist' activity is often, perhaps more often than not, performed for untheorized reasons and judged in untheorized ways.

Theory and practice in general

Theory is often asserted to be important. In a variety of ways, from the common sense and unreflected to the sophisticated and self-consciously philosophical, we are urged that what is wrong with our practice is remediable by a closer attention to theory.[9] I too believe theory to be significant and I want to try to describe why theory is a necessary part of practice and to place sociological theory in explicit relation to social practice.

Social theory is important because it is inevitable, and if we ignore the inevitable we are in the uncomfortable position of willing our own ignorance. We are all social theorists both in everyday life and in what we may choose, perhaps falsely, to mark off as our 'professional' lives. At its crudest this may simply mean that we all have value systems or ideologies which penetrate our work. At a more discriminating level this means that we actually use theories which are usually taken from somewhere else. We do not invent our theories. Not only are we all versions of the theorist but we are all versions of specific kinds of sociological, psychological, moral and political theorists who have, in the absence of any central collective concern with this theorizing activity, developed our choices and our partisanships in what is an inadequate arena. It must be inadequate if compared with the circumstances we could create for theoretical work. The argument goes then – sociological theory is of crucial importance as the vehicle of self-consciousness about our inevitable theorizing: making the implicit explicit.

All men are theoretical beings in so far as this involves them in abstraction, generalization, prediction, choice and decision-making and, so far as we know, all men do these things. One of the reasons for the recent attractiveness of phenomenological sociology is surely that it gives all men the status of theorist.

All men are practical and are involved in social action. Theory and practice are often seen as different logical orders[10] with different imperatives and importances. Yet we know they are connected. There are a number of common meanings given to the distinction. A series of commonsense dualisms seem to fit (e.g. intellectual/worker, manual work/brain work) and a technical and social division of labour has crystallized out around it. Theory is the rather despised half of the dichotomy ('oh, it's only theory' is a common criticism) yet embedded in the pair of terms is the fact that they are a duet and that they are indissolubly connected. That is, we know that theory must have an object. But common sense leaves the nature of the connections unexplicated beyond a denigration of each separated half ('ivory tower idealist' versus 'unreflective pragmatist').

Theory and practice are events and processes in a real world composed of matter and ideas. The relation between mind and matter is the fundamental dualism of all western philosophy. For the sociologist the strains of treating this as a practical matter have often resulted in the mystification of the relations between theory and practice. In science, the humanities, and the social disciplines, the tension between theorizing and practising is colonized by the activity of theory itself: the distinction or relation between theorizing and practising is seen as a theoretical one. This tends to provide more fuel for epistemological and philosophical argument. The relation is not treated as a practical one, and there are few examinations of the actual practical connection.[11]

Ideas and the organization of ideas, which comprise the theory world, are not enough. Thinking about thinking is not a prior activity to thinking about thinking about *something*[12] if only because practice, by its very nature, does not wait upon the resolution of theory. The constraints of the real world are too great to put off activity until all the great issues are settled. What this implies is that theory has a relationship to practice which is complicated by time. We cannot wait for ever for theoretical certainty yet we can wait. Thus, given that we will act whatever, our theory must be oriented to the inevitable action. The élitism, arrogance and false expertise which theorists often evince is in part due to their ignorance of the conditional and provisional character of their activity.

Man's activity has the outstanding characteristic that it is purposive.[13] Men have intentions which are simply ideas about what they can make happen. It is true that men are very often gripped by events which seem beyond their control, but in general our efforts are devoted, often unsuccessfully, to gripping the world and to being in control. This is a rather unfashionable sentiment in much of present-day sociology. Control is felt to be unworthy and fundamentally base – a kind of hubris. Planning, foresight and the prediction of consequences, however, are themselves an important motivation for the sciences and the social disciplines alike. The painful obviousness of the unintended consequences of our intended actions is the very reason for sociology. This is not a reduction of sociology to some crude engineering version of 'policy science'[14] and it is not to deny that sociology does provide ancillary aesthetic and intellectual satisfactions. But it is a reminder that sociology is deeply concerned to discuss the relation between ends and means, as well as ends themselves, and it is in this context that theory and practice must be seen.

The institutional contexts of knowledge and activity are also an important limiting factor in their relationship.[15] The growth of professions and of bureaucracies, the splitting and subsequent attempted reuniting of scholarship and activism have had profound effects on disciplines as ways of knowledge and definers of practice. The technical division of labour within all disciplines has a number of neglected implications for the impact of those disciplines on the enclosing society. In some disciplines it is true that the division between theorist and practitioner has all but disappeared for idiosyncratic reasons (e.g. astronomy). But in most, and in the social disciplines in particular, the distinction is a real one and the consequences of continuing role separation are serious. Gulfs open up in bodies of knowledge previously felt to be a unity. These often seem due more to the internal, often artificial, dynamics of the discipline than real responses to problems of knowledge and practice. Calling such sectarianism the growth of knowledge is using a very poor indicator indeed and in certain cases seems to inhibit any practice at all but further fission. Scientific revolutions and paradigm change[16] are not made of such stuff. Institutions and organizations have grown in such a way as not to permit pluralism, heterogeneity and possible co-operation in a discipline, but have turned it into an exclusive and bitter conflict where the private goals become winning and nothing else.

In general theory and practice have at best a pragmatic relationship and at worst are seen to be warring activities.

Theory and practice in science

Science, the magisterial standard of all our knowledge, is generally conceived as a kind of theory. The natural sciences function stereotypically as a measure of reliability, truth, usefulness and, in general, quality of what we say we know or even experience. The philosophy of science has developed polemical yet profound descriptions of what this important standard of science is[17] and a great deal of sociological theorizing has been devoted to anatomizing scientific knowledge-gaining procedures and in the process putting other disciplines within the social sciences and humanities in their 'proper' place. Within scientific theory science is seen as a body of ideas and a very limited single practice – namely experimentation – which feeds back on to those ideas. This theoretical view of science holds true across important debates.[18]

Yet science is more than ideas. It is profoundly a practice and concentrating on its idea-systems and how they have changed is as absurd as a complete view of science as is the history of technology and machines. Ironically this arrogant philosophizing is just as common among marxist sociologists who define themselves as very far away from the technical debates about scientific method as such.[19] Across the board the idealization of natural science has proscribed an examination of science as an institution which is relevant to theorizing about science. The sociology of scientists has remained a minor sub-branch of the sociology of professions or organizations as far as most theorists are concerned.[20]

Theory in science is conceived, at least by philosophers of science if not working scientists themselves, as sets of propositions asserting general relations between sets of phenomena or qualities of sets of phenomena. These are hypothetico-deductive in form. We ought here to distinguish between 'theories' – substantive hypotheses which account for and explain observed events in the physical world – 'meta-theory'[21] – metaphysical puzzles and problems which provide the boundaries which inspire theories – and 'theory' – the broadly accepted and explicit assumptions within which scientific activity can proceed. Theory, as conceived of here, is something like Kuhn's 'paradigms'[22] and includes methodology or theories of method. Scientists work within a broad theory which expresses values such as the value of empirical laws, prediction, the rejection of intuition and the propriety of hypothetico-deductive models.[23] These are the values of procedure and of acceptable knowledge. It is a body of ideal values to which scientists subscribe and it serves to give what they do a unified character. Very few scientists in a few select fields believe that they can be purely theoretical and still be scientists. Science cannot exist where explanation is posited which is not corrigible in some way by evidence.[24] *Exhibition* rather than theory is the hallmark of physical science and because of the importance of this (expressed how we will; falsifiability, testability, etc.) *within theory itself* there is a poorly developed technical division of labour around the theory–practice distinction within science. Theory means and requires practice. However, this practice has meant a limited range of activity in science's own terms. Theory in science has not embodied a fully socialized conception of practice.[25]

What would such a conception of socialized scientific practice tell us about science? At the very least it would orient us to looking beyond the enclosed world of scientific institutions. It would be an 'externalist' conception of practice.[26] The conventional externalist account would simply link science with technology, possibly making the distinction between 'pure' and 'applied' science and probably denying the interaction between the two. Recent pessimistic considerations of science, for instance that of Marcuse, have certainly viewed the two as connected. As he says:[27]

> Scientific-technical rationality and manipulation are welded together into new forms of social control. Can one rest content with the assumption that this unscientific outcome is the result of a specific societal *application* of science? I think that the general direction in which it came to be applied was inherent in pure science even where no practical purposes were intended.

Habermas views 'positivist' science as drenched with the values of a narrow, technical practicality. He sees science as a purely technically rooted cognitive interest and as a threat.[28] These are views which treat science as social practice but there is no attempt to break down the variety of functions of such practices. Yet more recent views see science as a force of production[29] and as a force of social control.[30] These views rely on the account of theory and practice – or rather scientific theory and industrial or military innovation – becoming historically separated. The marxist account of practice as the process of production or transformation requires an account of natural science practice which tries to transcend the internal logic of the progressive understanding of natural phenomena which is

9

embedded, albeit with different detailed implications, within any scientific theory. Science cannot judge the implications of its own practice because its theory excludes such considerations. So theory in science functions to unify scientists and to restrict their practice. This does not appear to be necessarily so.

What is practice in natural science, then? We are faced with a choice between an internalist and a sociological description. The internalist version is also limited by its own theory. A sociology of science looks at science's social practice governed by its own sociological theory. The concentration on the real effects of technology and science[31] attempts from a variety of theoretical positions to describe the full range of impacts and the variety of levels at which such impacts are felt. Sociological accounts of scientists' practices in different organizational contexts[32] reveal activity which would not be predicted by scientific theories or idealized accounts of the growth of scientific knowledge. Science interacts with dimensions of social power, hierarchy and bureaucracy: it does not completely transcend them regardless of what its theory directs it to do. This is not the aberration of science but is part of its real pattern of practice.

Scientific practice is not value free. It involves ethical choices (by commission or omission) but such choices are well-nigh smothered by its own theories. The iconic status not of scientific theory but of scientific practice is increasingly receiving well-merited attention.

The idealized version of the scientist[33] specifies a moral neutrality and a need to understand which serve to motivate scientific activity. It is in this sense that science serves as an ideology which has important consequences, many of which are wholly beneficial. The search for 'pure' understanding or knowledge is surely a virtue in its own right and it would be jejune to imagine that the methodologies attendant on such a belief have had wholly bad results. It is hard to see how the critical positions of a Marcuse or a Habermas transcend the constructive positions of science except by fiat.[34]

The relation between theory and practice in science has been a tabernacle for the social disciplines. Nothing said so far has reduced its moral power. All that has been noted only warns of a too easy understanding of science by reference to its theory's conception of its own practice.

The humanities

The attribution 'social *science*' is a clear indication of the prevailing cultural choice in the social disciplines. Sociologists wish to be scientists. Within institutions of higher education the humanities comprise a broad contrast discipline with an apparently different relation between theory and practice, but which might claim our attention. The crucial place of ideas in sociology[35] might nudge us towards looking at history, the classics and literary criticism as sources of self-understanding.

Historically the humanities have functioned publicly to inspire individual virtue in the members of an élite. As Plumb notes,[36] until the First World War establishment leaders relied upon the classics for civic morality, divinity for a source of aphorism and parable, history for models of heroes and patriots, and literature for the icing on the cake of the imagination. Popularly this function is thought to be extinct and this fact is used to explain the reduced power of the humanities to control education and influence policy-making. We have relegated the humanities to 'high' culture and side-tracked their exponents into a purely cultural élite who serve, along with practising artists, as sophisticated entertainers. As Gellner has noted,[37] we see the downgrading of the humanist intellectual in favour of the technocrat or policy scientist. This historical change reveals a great deal about the relation between theory and practice in the humanities.

Much of this startling reduction of the status and influence of the humanities may be attributable to the loss of belief in the autonomy of culture.[38] In a pre-technocratic time ideas and ideals were not only felt to reside in a small élite (and also, therefore, in their education) but were the foundation for their judgment of affairs. Virtues of various kinds as taught by the humanities were the motive and locus of policy in a publicly realized way (e.g. style, moralism, formalism). Institutional change was contemplated to conform with humanistic (especially scriptural) ideals, for instance in Poor Law reform. Texts of the time avow the pre-eminence of the cultural.[39]

The period since the First World War has seen a decline in the public and political reliance on culture as at all relevant, though there are indications of a reaction to this recently.[40] There may be a number of ways of explaining this change: the demystification and rationalization inherent in an accelerating rate of scientific growth; political changes in élite composition and closure; the promotion of 'popular' culture; the demands of capitalist social organization for a cultural contribution to the reproduction of the relations of production and to consumption. However it is explained it is apparent that culture is now powerfully believed to have nothing to say about fundamental problems and issues. Structure is seen to drag culture behind it. Isolated humanist intellectuals who continue to deny an ideal-less materialism are exceptions.

Theory and practice in the humanities has changed as the belief in the autonomy of the cultural enterprise has changed. Theory in the past was dogmatic and textual and primarily exegetic rather than hermeneutic.[41] Practice was, in effect, the total social behaviour of the élite individual and the ability in social and political life to manifest arcane wisdom, and follow classic example. Scholarship was only a small and idiosyncratic part of practice. Much more significant was the shaping of the potential for leadership. Hence the important part of practice carried on in public schools as well as universities. At the widest level practice was the élite intervention in society in the defence of civilized values through the personal qualities of the humanist individual.

The relation between theory and practice becomes more obscure and more complex with the decline of the humanities. The reaffirmation of a high culture in the face of the absorption of habits of aesthetics and value judgment which had previously been the exclusive preserve of the élite was one development. The cultivation of a select group of people with 'superior capacities for discrimination',[42] especially in the field of literary criticism, seems like the development of a rather redundant fine tuner. The old theory embodying values derived from 'great books' becomes overlaid with a function of guarding 'the word' from vulgarization. The exclusiveness of the old political élite has become transformed into an almost religious cultural protectionism – from the philosopher king to the guardian of the scrolls. This position mimics in miniature the old theory–practice division. The complication arises in the involvement of the humanities in the creation of popular culture. Here the old theory concerns about value become diluted with theories of communication. The great thinkers become redundant as the new theorists of communication (e.g. McLuhan) appear to give more leverage to concern with the popularizing of ideas. Practice becomes the ability to get ideas across regardless of what those ideas are or what their source. The theory–practice relation begins to resemble the technocratic theory–practice relation, that is the belief in restricted technical tasks combined with huge ramifications of those tasks which are ignored by the theory.

Theory and practice in the humanities now is ruptured not between theory and practice themselves but between two broad types of theory-and-practice constellation. The fault is the line marking the concern with élitism and populism. This split we shall see is mirrored and magnified in the social disciplines which only rarely turn to the humanities for an improved understanding of the contradictions we all now labour under.

Practical sociology

The history of sociology as expounded to sociologists has been made into the history of theory. The history of theory in science and the humanities is also read off as the history of those disciplines. This is inadequate, as has already been noted. The history of a practical sociology becomes invisible for lack of use, while the continual rehearsal of a theoretical sociology leads up to only one kind of performance – theory – and one kind of action – theoreticism.

There is a peculiar poverty of theoretical work in that area which we might call traditional applied sociology.[43] The conceptual vulgarity and pragmatism which we see in this area is not, however, a necessary condition but is contingent upon the particular work evident, especially that work produced in the

13

USA in the 1960s. In collections of the work[44] accounts of consultancy roles are described in various institutional settings and a picture drawn of the sociologist as a researcher who accepts the goals of his employer, largely uncritically. The definitions of social problems are unquestioningly seen as administrative, the terms in which they are posed are built into the research done and the methods of dealing with them are within the administrator's catalogue 'the possible'. There is little evidence that researchers have any conception of the levels of social practice or realization of their assumptions of basic value consensus. The explicit theoretical work which does exist in these collections, rather like the very thin slices of bread in a sandwich, is devoted to classifying the roles of the sociologist as 'clinician', 'engineer', 'consultant' or 'broker'.

The absorption of the social sciences into government and administration during the 1950s and 1960s obviously delimited acceptable roles for the applied sociologist. What is interesting is the way in which being employed as an applied sociologist became prestigious in academic terms: became first a respectable model for the development of sociology as a discipline, and then a despised stereotype against which a rarefied academicism reacted.

Applied sociology has at least to pretend to a theoretical component. In many ways the attempts to explicate a theoretical position which leave the role of the consultant unproblematic are more distasteful than the a-theoreticism of the consultants themselves.[45] This process is still going on.[46]

In America the absence of a theoretical tradition which made the theory–practice relationship its main focus goes part of the way to explaining the peculiar nature of American applied sociology. In Britain the historical development was more complex.[47] While the imitation of the American pattern of applied sociology is probably important (in much the same way as the expansion of sociology departments in Britain in the 1960s seemed imitative of America) there are undoubtedly more local and specific reasons for the lack of development of a theory–practice concern. However it is explained, what is apparent is that there has been no convincing development of sociology as an interventionist discipline which would provide a real alternative to a purist concern with epistemological and philosophical issues. The question now is – is such a discipline a contradiction in terms, which has thus been justly ignored, or is it a possible option for the development of sociology?

Theoretical sociology

We should also consider the history of sociological theory. The major debate might be about whether this history is to be seen as one of paradigm change (progressive or regressive)[48] or the continual redramatization of old and inevitable antinomies. Such a choice may not be immediately apparent in the many available histories of sociological theory.[49] But with the recent explosion in the apparent variety of theory positions it becomes important in order to judge whether our theory has actually changed. The broad movements since, say, Comte may reveal a move to a progressive, encompassing theory marked by important transitions in the work of Marx or Durkheim for example. Or it may illustrate the oscillations between necessary choices which social scientists must make with recent fashions merely pointing to an increasing rate of oscillation.

The role of theory in sociology is complex. As in other disciplines it motivates, unifies and directs inquiry. But it also divides the discipline into 'schools', acts as a vehicle for moral demonstration and, unlike in many other disciplines, functions as a kind of disciplinary world on its own apparently unconcerned with practice at all, and within which a rather artificial and precocious internal division of labour can work itself out. This is a comparatively recent development and has been parasitic upon the self-conscious turning away from practice. The concern with the 'founding fathers' in sociology should not be seen simply as a concern with the history of ideas. The narrative of the developments of the various national sociologies has not only been concerned with ideas.[50] The chronology of theory which is the basic material upon which the social theory world feeds is poor nourishment and the starved body of theory spasmodically jerking towards each new epistemological development is evidence of this. How then should we consider sociological theory?

The term 'sociological theory' is used promiscuously to refer sometimes to any generalized statement about thought whatever, and sometimes to only generalized statements about social life with deductive consequences which are empirically testable. Both slack and rigid uses of social theory, at this stage of the game, build out of our awareness the possible range of uses of sociological theory. Following Glucksmann[51] we can identify five kinds of statements under the rubric 'sociological theory': (a) epistemology, or statements about the grounds of knowledge and the safeness of making kinds of statements about the world (what sort of knowledge is achievable?); (b) philosophy, or whole world views which incorporate values and create the boundaries of social phenomena (including theorizing activity itself) in thought; (c) 'theory', strictly understood as substantive hypotheses accounting for and explaining observed events; (d) methodology, or prescriptions about the rectitude of types of methods of research; (e) description, or demarcating 'fields of study' as homogeneous objects. These, as Glucksmann notes, are in descending order of abstraction though not necessarily of determinacy. Historically speaking conventional debates in sociological theory academies are conducted between protagonists at the level of (c) and antagonists who shift fluidly up and down the other levels. Very quickly theoretical debates become confrontations where 'winning' becomes a tactic of travelling to different and preferably more abstract levels of theory than one's opponent. Thus quite often what appear to be rival theories are merely the products of the theorists themselves arguing with different senses of the word 'theory'. Examples might be confrontations between dialectical theory and conflict theory or phenomenological sociologies versus functionalist sociologies. The end result is a squabbling incestuousness which activists despise and reject and in the rejecting condemn theory itself.

The trouble with much of the debate in the theory world conducted under such auspices is that it seems to be of little interest to 'practical' people and appears to be scholasticist dialogues, sermons or alienating polemics. I think it revealing that on sociology degree courses theory is often the most apparently irrelevant and tedious area for students. This is because theory has become divorced from practice in the discussion of theory itself. Occasionally theory is linked with empirical research and the claim is then made for relevance,[52] but research is only one rather idiosyncratic form of practice. It is not often that as a first priority theory is linked with practice in general and with the specific forms which practice takes in our society.

Identity of the 'crisis'

Sociology as a discipline with both an ideological and an institutional existence is increasingly riven by internecine strife. Dispute, schism, factionalism and distrust characterize sociology mainly because of the enervating fission which has distinguished recent developments. This hostility, rather than the heterogeneity, derives from theory which is concerned only with issues of theory. It is part of the message of this book that theory which recognizes the primacy of practice in theorizing (and this means much more than being 'reflexive' in Gouldner's terms)[53] would help to unite a discipline in ways which a call for the simple abandonment of this or that position or the promotion of this or that position could not.[54] At the moment few teachers, students, researchers and users of sociology can doubt there is an identity crisis which began with an ideological crusade and is becoming an institutional enfeeblement.

It is not the inability of sociology's users and practitioners to make realistic demands which is the fundamental condition of this crisis, though this is relevant, so much as the internal conditions of the discipline. The analogy with a declining church is striking: both faith and works are needed but the theology and the organization are preoccupied with questions of correct interpretation and internal status demands. No church can survive this except in a state of siege. The prognosis for a sociology encumbered with a dead weight of theoretical dispute is poor.

Why is it that today more than at any other time both the demand for and the failure of social theory within a world of social problems is so great? Is it the political blindness and the pragmatic self-concern of the policy-makers which is to blame or is it the fault of theory itself?

17

There are numerous classifications of types of sociological theory. All they demonstrate is the schism and fragmentation within sociology generally. Effectively there is no 'discipline' of sociology to which one can go and demand a contribution to the definition and solution of social problems – though all mutually hostile schools of theory will be only too happy to provide a condemnation of present arrangements which will probably call itself a 'critique'.

Many of the recent classifications of theory appear similar in that under different labels they divide sociological theory into two varieties. For the sake of argument only we might label these varieties 'orthodox' and 'radical'. I think that this distinction is common and powerful among many social science students and to an important degree among young planners, social workers, teachers and some lawyers. It is a confusion but it has come, as a theoretical construct, to exert a real influence on users' views of possible goals and means. It is a case study in the creation of practical incapacity by bad theory. A characterization, perhaps a caricature, of these two positions is useful. 'Radical' sociology over the last decade can be seen as a conflation of a variety of incompatible versions of marxism, a reading of phenomenological sociology as biographical relativism, variants of existential psychology which refuse to recognize human misery as a possible target for social action and finally a distaste for determinism and the methodologies appropriate to it. These versions of the radical sit very uneasily together and in a bathwater made so murky by their intermingling several promising babies have been almost dissolved, let alone obscured. Yet plainly radical sociology functions as an allegiance. Unfortunately the net result is either quietism or a very generalized form of radical activity which, as Cohen notes[55] is insensitive to immediate suffering and cannot begin to reconcile, in moral terms, immediate needs and long-term goals. I fully realize that the increasing fragmentation of sociology is resulting in proliferating sub-categories of radicals and that they fiercely condemn each other. But on a broad view they share more than they dispute.

'Orthodox' sociology, on the other hand, is a grab-bag of

logical positivism, a concern for substantive social problems defined in administrative terms, a belief in the determinacy of social structure and a belief that interpersonal relations and sensibility are essentially superficial. Orthodox sociology is a shopping list of more or less discrete theoretical topics which formed syllabi and which were espoused by prestigious researchers in the 1950s and early 1960s. These broadly claimed a technocratic or scientific basis for the discipline. It now functions as a banner for those who wish to claim authority by moral or political character.

Plainly these two categories are neither exhaustive or exclusive. Plainly there is nearly as much confusion, separation and incompatibility within the two camps as there is between them. Yet the division endures, has effects and becomes more concrete. Shifts into philosophy and formalism or into naked activism are often attempts to escape dilemmas of allegiance of this kind.

There is a justified wariness about chiliastic crisis-mongers. The apocalypse which is sure to follow unless the prophet's words are heeded seldom measures up to what we now think of as a true crisis (famine, war, disease, etc. – that is misery in Barrington Moore's terms). Let us be clear about the scale of the 'crisis' of sociology. It is simply the destruction of a potential. This potential in sociology for helping in the relief of suffering and the promotion of sensibility is important in a society which seems to have overcome the most fundamental problems of the production of the raw materials for continuing life but has not achieved any measure of the quality or value of that life.

At the moment sociology's potential is still dormant and the hibernation is encouraged by the travails of its users. If we disaggregate this category of 'sociology users' we will see that there is little use or enjoyment of sociology by anyone except professional theory-mongers. Its impact on policy-making in central and local government is so indirect as to be unknowable. The official sociology embodied in the policy research of the state apparatus is, where inconvenient or embarrassing, ignored with impunity. Whether as specialist units within local government or the civil service or as paid consultants, sociologists cannot appear to deliver knowledge with sufficient authority to begin to approach major social problems over which the state exercises jurisdiction. Other 'consumers' of sociology have used only market research or a dubious form of futurology and wherever possible attempt to dismiss the discipline. Researchers in the social problems field work with the certain awareness that the products of their research will have no effect on policy whatever, and little effect on social action.[56]

In terms of education the effect of sociology on students is depressing in that it squashes their impulses to contribute to the social world beyond the sociology profession. It fails as training, having no firm discipline grounded in the connection between theory and practice, rather than their separation, and it fails as education, providing neither personal enjoyment nor a sense of the expansion of understanding and competence. Sociology fails students not because of the way it is taught, but because what is taught is drained of 'practical' implication. The largely empirical conclusions of the sub-areas of sociology are left as free-standing criticisms rather than as stepping stones towards reconstruction united in theory and prescriptive implication. Theory courses are taught as ends in themselves or as arenas for the practice of style. Major exceptions to these criticisms are courses taught with the emphasis on 'praxis' from a marxian viewpoint, but these are subject, as we shall see later, to spirals of mystification which stem from a lack of a time-sense of practice and social problems. Theory in sociology courses is the *locus classicus* of the alienation of the bulk of sociology students: the very alienation which is the main topic of discussion in these courses.

We are left with a position in which, especially in teaching and research, sociologists construct a social world which prohibits their effective action and in which they condemn themselves to a purely internal dialogue.

Sociological theory has an important part to play in remedying this situation (by no means the only part of course). Motivating and moralizing are certainly important parts of the theoretical enterprise and sociology needs to exploit the values of compassion, activism, and the desire to help rather than cynicism, academicism and quietism. Sociology has the potential for being a truly popular approach to the need of people who suffer problems to achieve an analytical grasp of them. This has been explored with varying degrees of success, particularly in the fields of urban reform and community work, and to a lesser degree within the fields of legal problems, crime and deviancy. It is also a potential expertise. Sociological theory must grasp the nettles of the relation between theory and practice and the relation between hierarchy and the division of labour. The social disciplines, unlike the physical and natural sciences, have no arcanum. The choice facing sociology now is whether to search for one (perhaps even to create one) by philosophical speculation, or to attempt a grip on a world of pressing and immediate problems.

2 Disciplines and professions

Knowledge is not autonomous. Neither is it totally socially determined. The sociology of knowledge, where it can ignore its own epistemological difficulties, is the attempt to describe the social conditions for the production and sustenance of what we take to be knowledge.[1] In doing this it tries to sort out how autonomous and how determined bodies of knowledge are. If we believe that ideas are either spontaneous and self-generating or only grow out of other ideas we would also be driven to believe that knowledge was an autonomously developing realm of social phenomena unanchored in the material conditions and the social demands of life. Alternatively if we believe that all ideas are only reflections of the conditions under which they arise or are somehow only 'called forth' by those social conditions we must see knowledge as the product of social organization. In the first case we must ignore the power of society and believe only in the power of the intellect: in the second the intellect is abandoned and we have great difficulty in understanding invention, innovation and discovery. Few sociologists would hold such crude idealist and materialist positions nowadays, but the 'middle way' does not easily provide a plausible general account of the link between knowledge as such and knowledge as a form of work.[2] What we are interested in is the way in which knowledge which is organized as a form of work, used in occupations and displayed as a basis of expertise, authority and status derives from and conditions knowledge which is the product of the most dispassionate inquiry of which we are capable. We would be foolish to imagine that there was no such thing as some kind of intellectual autonomy (or even some blurred inherent logic to knowledge itself), mediated and entangled as it may appear to be.

The cutting edge of the general relationship between theory and practice appears in the precise relationship between disciplines and professions, or between institutionalized and organized discourses and occupations. This is to broach the profound sociological topic of the relations between the social division of labour and knowledge. I do not want to suggest that knowledge is the source of the particular and visible division of labour in our society[3] or that some deep logic to social life structures the division of labour which itself structures knowledge,[4] but it can be seen that there is a mutual penetration of the organization of knowledge, especially in universities but also in other institutions, and the use to which that knowledge is put – not just the implied practical object of particular researches but the function which such knowledge has for particular groups. If there is such a thing as intellectual autonomy then it must be seen against the background of the conditioning and control of organized intellectual life by a variety of groups in society. For knowledge to grow (change, move, etc.) we must be able to understand and separate the intellectual and institutional conditions of organized knowledge in the past.

The development of sociology and economics as organized discourses, or disciplines, has occurred contemporaneously with their increasing use in particular kinds of social intervention. The shift from autonomous scholarship to state-sponsored administrative science has obscured the alternative possible contributions of sociological thought to experienced problems. Rescuing these institutional conditions, which will encourage the intellectual growth of sociology, will revive the real range of contributions that the discipline can make. The forms of sociology which are now appropriate for only particular professional groups do not circumscribe the discipline, neither do they allow the pluralism which is constitutive of this particular discipline.

In chapters 3, 4 and 5 an attempt is made to illustrate the specific relevance of sociological theorizing to particular 'professional' interventionist practices. This is done in order to show the importance of a range of theorizing which itself depends upon a commitment to pluralism in the discipline of sociology. In this chapter the general relationship between disciplines and occupations is briefly introduced. In both discussions the faith placed in intellectual autonomy by those working within the relevant disciplines is contrasted with the pragmatic interests of those groups who will use disciplines and pretend that their own self-serving requirements necessarily match the needs of the problems with which they ostensibly deal.

Disciplines

The commonsense definition of a discipline might be of a branch of learning which has a recognized place in an institution of education and research and which has enough writers and readers who believe they are engaged in a dialogue to justify library space and categorization. In this sense disciplines are socially chartered and authorized bodies of knowledge and personnel. Such organized knowledges have developed historically. Disciplines are not 'natural' or 'real' representations of the subject-matters of their knowledges; that is, they are a mixture of responses to what are taken to be obdurate slabs of reality and responses to changing political, moral and technical conditions.[5] Disciplines have both an ideological and an institutional existence. But in commonsense terms they are believed to be only knowledges.

Academics and scholars who necessarily hold to an implicit theory of disciplines presumably believe that their disciplines are in some sense *just* bodies of knowledge – systematized collections of propositions or observations about a 'subject' which has an ontological status separate from other 'subjects'. Their discipline is also unified by very high-level methodologies. At this level debates about paradigms become debates about disciplinary membership and identity.[6] The very term 'discipline' implies rules and the nature of a discipline as a community of rule-followers is one which is traded upon but seldom examined by academics.

The location of disciplines within academies is also significant. Although many writers now recognized as of high status in their discipline (possibly even creating it) worked away from universities, their work depended upon organized scholarship, teaching and publication, and the maintenance of specialized audiences. Universities have their own organizational dynamics dependent upon their connection with power élites and their autonomy from the state. Departments are founded and particular disciplines encouraged or proscribed in part for organizational reasons.[7]

However we wish to describe the institutional correlates of disciplines, what is plain is that disciplines are not just autonomous bodies of knowledge and learning which are the untrammelled expression of cognitive faculties. They are social and cultural and in a sophisticated sense political. As the state increasingly controls or at least licences academies and research organizations it has a great deal of potential control over the creation and destruction of disciplines. The existence of 'management studies' or 'business studies' attests to this. Spasmodically debate, especially within the state administrative apparatus, is concerned with the conservative and retarding effects of disciplinary divisions, and appeals are made for a recasting of traditional disciplines. In a strong form this is done by the invention of whole new disciplines (e.g. 'public administration'); in a weak form by bleating about inter-, trans- and cross-disciplinary requirements or problem-centred approaches. These are not arguments denying disciplinary boundaries as such and their propriety: merely about the convenience of those that exist at the moment for administrators.

But where do disciplines come from? Is their existence justified in some way by their source? Do the disciplinary boundaries we now live with reflect real distinctions in the world? How do we account for different disciplinary formations in different societies? Questions like these require us to probe a little deeper into the foundations of the division of academic knowledge. One of the most valuable recent approaches to the fundamental constitution of disciplines, and subsequently sciences, is that of the marxist Louis Althusser[8] which is made specially accessible and clear in the work of Therborn.[9] Sciences are founded on theoretical systems which 'discover/produce' 'patterns of determination'[10] which are held to account for the behaviour of extra-theoretical phenomena. The social sciences do not emerge as a result of a penetration into the unknown produced by new instruments. A

25

discipline becomes a science when it produces a 'theoretical object' to act upon a 'real object'. Many disciplines do not possess a theoretical object, which is 'a set of concepts developed to account for the various real objects which the science is claimed to analyse'.[11] Such disciplines are not sciences and have only an institutional distinctiveness. The point to be emphasized here is the concentration of these marxists on the theoretical basis of disciplines which can claim to be sciences. As Therborn puts it:

> The empirical study of, say, political institutions, is no more the sufficient condition of a real political science than the observation of birds with binoculars is of the science of ornithology, even where the birdwatcher is attached to an institution called a 'university'.[12]

That is, sciences are not the observation and classification of empirical phenomena: they are a theoretical constitution.[13] The elaboration of a science from any generalized discourse requires intellectual skills and the formation of a division of labour. That is, disciplines, whether achieving the status of sciences or not, are the product of particular societies in a particular historical period. Thus, to take Therborn's own example, economics emerged as a discourse on the new commercial capitalism, and sociology emerged as the study of politics after the bourgeois revolution, attempting to deal with the problems of capitalism while under the shadow of a militant working-class movement and the threat of revolutionary socialism.[14] Organized knowledge is historically specific, or, if we prefer, socially relative.

The importance of such arguments is that they clarify the sophisticated determinist position on the growth and variation of disciplines. The 'discovery' of new sciences through the 'discovery/production' of 'new' sets of concepts can only be described from this position as epistemological ruptures, breaks or revolutions. It cannot be explained because the autonomous power of intellectual development has been abandoned for a determinist, albeit complex, position. Ultimately a discipline's existence is in some way called forth by the deep structure of social development and its precise forms and character can be explained by accounting for the place of academies and academics.

In looking at this approach we are forced to come to terms with the institutional conditions of disciplines. We may not wish to accept that the methodologies, theories and insights of particular disciplines can be explained only in a functionalist way, but we cannot ignore the institutional circumstances of their elaboration. Therborn's view is that sociology's character, especially in its classical period (roughly 1880–1920), and perhaps even more so now, is explained partly by the marginal character of its proponents who, unlike economists, were not related directly to the 'hegemonic fraction' of the bourgeoisie but were part of an alienated bourgeois intelligentsia. Similarly Eisenstadt's and Curelaru's view that the recent increase in density and quantity of sociological communities (that is academic departments of sociology) without a corresponding institutionalization of their own control over their resources helps to explain present tendencies to schism and fragmentation.[15] Both of these are just examples of how the form and content of a discipline are incomprehensible without some understanding of their social conditions as well as their intellectual pedigree. The distinguishing features of a discipline must be sought in the system of relations in which it is embedded and not just within the complex of intellectual activities which is its façade.

Disciplines are embedded in universities. Universities are central to the social organization characteristic of the intellectual life of western Europe and America, especially since the late nineteenth century, and they have formed an intellectual community with a partial and variously autonomous culture and organizational character.[16] The secularization of academies and their incorporation into the state towards the end of the last century was the setting for the classical period of sociology.[17] The accommodation of a potentially critical sociology at this time to a developing nationalism and the use of the university as an agency of national integration set the ground rules for sociology's academic respectability. Later in the 1930s, as Gouldner notes,[18] the American university provided a financially and culturally insulated haven from the crises of the depression within which Talcott Parsons could produce apparently socially detached monuments of what has since proved to be seminal theoretical

27

work. In other words both the setting of the modern university and its internal characteristics condition the shape of disciplines. New ideas are not enough to found new disciplines, as one study of the establishment of a new discipline shows.[19] There must also exist the institutional means of establishing a new intellectual identity. Scholarship and the disinterested pursuit of truth are not, of course, pure inventions but as styles of intellectual work they are not independent of the changing conditions which are claimed to sustain them. The recent changes in university structures and independence, especially their increasing public inspection, have opened up a wider range of roles for academic sociologists, changed career patterns, and altered the isolation of academics from wider social and economic shifts.

Disciplines are used and knowledge is organized as a form of work by groups other than licensed academics.

Disciplines and professions

The division of labour is a core theme in sociologists' speculations about industrial societies. With the theme of hierarchy it probably dominates nearly all macro-sociological concern. Work and workers are divided up into categories in societies which appear to be partly technical and partly cultural. These categories come to be reified and have important effects on the organization of social life in general. An increasing preoccupation in this area is with those occupational groups which we might call and who themselves bid for the label 'professional'.[20] We are especially interested in professionals because they are groups of workers which make claims to a number of special statuses, superior to those of other occupations, founded upon the knowledge base of their work and their disciplinary identifications. They are thus both a revealing example, and an important model, of how theory can lead to practice.

Professionals themselves claim high rewards, status and effectiveness in the world of practice. The word 'professional' is a term in common use of estimation and prestige. There is an ideology of 'professionalism' through which some groups maintain already achieved control and independence (for instance lawyers) and other groups try to increase authority and rewards (for instance social workers and town planners). But this use of the term, embedded in practice itself, obscures in its mundane familiarity the place of such occupations within society and the conditions of such social differentiation. This ideology of professionalism has been so powerful that until recently sociologists themselves were content to analyse it without inquiring into the system of social relations in which it was embedded. Sociologists have for a long time accepted that there was substance to professionals' own claims that there was something special about professions, something which marked them off from other jobs and which could operate as some sort of standard which other groups increasingly tried to attain (hence 'quasi-professionals' for example).[21] They have been guilty of accepting the ideology of professionalism at face value. It is not just cynical to argue that in part this has been due to the attempted professionalization of the sociologist himself as a means of authenticating his discipline.[22] Sociologists are enmeshed more than most in the interactional tangle of discipline and profession. The ideology of professionalism was recast by uncritical sociologists into two broad explanatory forms.[23] First was the 'trait' explanation which accounted for the specialness of professions by some inherent characteristic of practice, such as skill, or some intrinsically restricted aspect of learning, such as the mastery of difficult concepts or developing memory. Second was the 'functional' approach which explained the high status and rewards of professions by their functional importance in society and the essential and important work they did. Both of these approaches search the profession/professional complex for some characteristic to justify the elevated status gained by certain occupations. They are interested in the occupational activity itself in the vain hope of providing a model of theory/practice which is essentially fixed within the knowledge and skill area − that is a technical and essentialist definition of professionalism. But this kind of quest is a highly restricted venture. Professions are occupations. They are outcomes of the division of labour which is itself a fundamental form of social differentiation. What sociologists should be interested in, as Johnson notes,[24] is the basis of occupational variation and the historically specific forms of the institutional control of the various occupations. There seems little in the way of traits or functional importances which are located only in those occupations which for historical reasons have come to be successfully called professions. Skill and importance are generally continuously distributed in work as a whole and not discontinuous attributes of only some kinds of activity.

Recently a number of sociologists have sharply questioned the basis of the designation 'profession' and the role professions play in society.[25] Professionalism, says Johnson, is a historically specific form of the institutional control of an occupation. It is a method, typically, of colleague control, rather than, for instance, client or paymaster control of work activity. Thus the traditional professions, law and medicine, are occupational groups sociologically remarkable, not for their knowledge but for their freedom from outside control and the extent of their authority over their own work processes. This autonomy is historically explainable and is institutionalized over time.

Teachers, social workers and town planners who wish to become professionalized cannot, of course, because of their historical lack of collegiate control and they can only emulate the ideological trappings of the old professions. Put bluntly, there is no essential quality of their work, knowledge, training, function or social importance which gives professions their high status; only the fact that they have maintained control over their own work. The maintenance of monopoly and the strategies of social closure in occupations are now what exercise many sociologists.[26]

This view of professions raises a number of questions about the use and appeal to disciplines by professions and their public reliance on knowledge as the support for their special status and as part of their strategies of social closure. Johnson's approach comes close to relegating professional knowledge to peripheral status, though this is remedied in a determinist way in his later work.[27] In general the appeal by professionals to their knowledge base operates to mystify the nature of their practice, their relations with their clients and with threatening groups.[28] More especially the professional's public reliance on knowledge both threatens and protects occupational self-control. In order to understand this contradictory relationship we should grasp the dual character of knowledge itself. On the one hand knowledge may be transmissible, on the other hand it may be arcane. The work of Jamous and Peloille[29] describes how these two characteristics may be considered to be in a ratio in any occupation. That is, for example, the established professions will stress the inscrutable and esoteric aspects of professional identity (charisma, ascription, initiation) rather than those aspects which can be straightforwardly transmitted (disciplines).

Disciplines, then, are only one part of knowledge and to the extent that reliance is placed upon them as the knowledge base the occupation in question will have revealed the transmissible basis of its expertise and also will have rendered itself vulnerable to the routinization and rationalization which all such codified knowledge obviously permits. The systematization of knowledge within universities and its use as a basis for certification ensures the openness of the knowledge-users to bureaucratic intervention.[30] To the extent that the indeterminate quality of relevant knowledge is stressed, what Jamous and Peloille call the 'virtualities',[31] occupational control is protected behind a screen of mystification which treats professional knowledge as a matter of special experience rather than learning.

Such an approach certainly complicates a view that there is an inherent logic to knowledge which itself dictates the division of labour and is especially evident now in increasing professionalization. The very reliance on disciplines is the factor which renders occupational self-control unlikely, yet it is the invention and continued fragmentation of disciplines which provide an opportunity for occupational specialization to attempt independence and authority via professionalization. Thus disciplines are not the source of professionalization but are its camouflage. Disciplines will not yield occupational authority. The importance we give them then must not rest on their contribution to special status for some occupations but on their functions and effects as defined by the disciplines themselves.

How are we to account for the variable use of disciplines by professions, and on what basis can we give an account of the future links between disciplines and professions? In other words, if there is no clear causal link between disciplinary developments (which we have already seen are not themselves pure cognitive developments) and so-called professionalization, how do we theoretize such changes in the division of labour? Johnson criticizes a Weberian approach which accentuates the inherent rationality of technique and knowledge and market processes. This, he says, cannot account sociologically for the differentiation of groups in society, and merely describes the changes in class structure in terms which themselves must be explained. He proposes a marxist approach in which he says the imperatives of the capitalist mode of production provide the basis for theoretizing the very existence of such groups as professionals and 'the new middle class'.[32] In his proposed approach the variable reliance on disciplines and non-transmissible knowledge is determined by the fundamental factor for all social analysis: for Johnson, the structure of the mode of production. Presumably although a marxist might be wary of attributing the very form and content of knowledge itself to the mode of production (except in such a mediated way as not to be marxist in any recognizable sense any more), he might argue that the division of labour which is so attributable itself exerts a force on disciplinary developments. The vulnerability of universities and academies to enclosing power structures is marked in their responses to demands for particular skills and credentials. The increase in professions is associated with the rise of the modern university in a reciprocal relationship of authentication and legitimation.

We are faced with two kinds of logic to explain the division of labour. One is the logic inherent in the formal, cognitive properties of knowledge itself. The other is the logic of transcendent laws of social development which incorporate and engulf knowledge. Both appear to operate. To deny a degree of cognitive autonomy which can ease or hinder specialization seems foolish.

Sociology, expertise and the intellectual

What is sociology's position as a discipline used by professions? There are no professions which publicly claim to base themselves upon sociology as a discipline but many use the knowledge provided by sociologists and thus depend upon its theoretical propriety. A number of occupations, such as social work and planning, depend upon sociology for a great deal of their knowledge. It appears that sociology acts as a servicing mechanism for the interventionist professions whether the sociologists like it or not, and regardless of the self-assigned role which is sometimes apparent in sociology of providing pure scholarship in an institutional vacuum. Increasingly the formal debates in the discipline ignore the embeddedness of sociology not just within a world of individual subjects who are themselves lay sociologists but within a constellation of organized moral and technical interests. If sociology, and thus its theory, are inevitably used, sociologists need some self-assessment of their intellectual and institutional position, their own place within the developing division of labour and the effects of their knowledge.

Sociologists are not professionals.[33] They have only the most vestigial of the ideological trappings of occupational self-control. Their status as a discipline with intellectual distinctiveness is often criticized[34] though its institutional formation now seems clear. Other disciplines in a similar position, notably in the social sciences, economics, have evolved the role, via the patronage of the state, of 'expert', heavily involved in an advisory capacity and claiming an authority based almost solely upon the cognitive validity of the knowledge and its pertinence to government and organization. In so far as the putative subject-matter of economists is also taken to be the fundamental concern of the state and its apparatus, expertise without professionalism becomes an idiosyncratic status granted to academics as a means of incorporation into the state.[35] As Gerver and Bensman recognised,[36] expertise is a conferred quality donated by other groups for their own purposes. Where a discipline appears to provide knowledge which promises control (of the natural and social worlds) to the user and where the guardians of that discipline for historical reasons have no collegiate control over the use of that knowledge, the academics will become licensed and retained experts as a means of status mobility and protection.[37]

Sociology, unlike economics, has not had this quality conferred on it and thus its detachment from the state and its lack of incorporation is greater than either professions or expertises. Sociologists must cast around for another role which will give them status and which will authenticate their academic position in a situation where they have no autonomous power and no influential patron. Two roles which are often adopted and are attempts at authentication by appeal to the traditional organization of knowledge or to other disciplines now effectively dead, are of 'critic' and 'scholar'. Both of these roles are loose versions of a more inclusive role, that of 'intellectual', which for many non-marxist sociologists is a fundamental part of the division of labour with an almost natural rather than social basis. That is, for sociology with a respectable pedigree in the history of thought and ideas but with a weak institutional basis in the universities (growing quickly, recently, and for peculiar reasons of fashion), the legitimacy sought is from a moral value and an associated social role thought to transcend both fashion and state patronage. In some way the role of intellectual is thought to be more profound and less historically transitory than that of professional or expert. This may hide the simple fact that sociology cannot provide knowledge which is reliably useful for governments as a means of social control and thus it has no extra-academic resources to protect its status.

Sociologists have two models of the intellectuals as a definable part of the division of labour to exploit. The first and most appealing description is that made most famous by Mannheim in 1936[38] and traded upon by academics since.[39] This is the view of intellectuals as an unanchored, relatively classless stratum, unified by education and through education able to surmount the bias to which all other class-based members of society are subject. This free-floating intelligentsia thus has a structural position of relative autonomy and the ability to be relatively objective. Intellectuals are thus given a very special and honoured status indeed as well as a moral responsibility for guarding the holy grail of knowledge, pursued as it is by warring factions. Intellectuals occur in all societies. They are seen to serve a basic social need for the creation of a sense of coherence and orderliness through their control over symbols and their penetration of immediate concrete experience.[40]

The second account, most obvious in the relevant writings of the Italian marxist Gramsci,[41] places the intellectuals firmly in the arena of the class struggle. For Gramsci 'traditional' intellectuals have the pedagogic function of maintaining and disseminating a cultural world view which is part of the ruling class's foundation of power. They maintain 'hegemony' by pedagogy. Traditional intellectuals assert an unfounded historical continuity and an independence as a stratum of society in order to protect the constitution of knowledge as their own 'property'. Their origin and their historic function is sought in their connection with the élite. They are in no way socially unattached or the possessors of some relatively independent truth but are simply the servants of power. Gramsci held that there are 'organic' intellectuals who do not pretend to this autonomy but deliberately serve the revolutionary class as organizers and constructors of the political party which provides the leadership for that class. These must be separated from the 'traditional' intellectuals.

Sociologists denied other roles have found both conceptions of the intelligentsia attractive. The first Mannheimian view provides a rationale for the existence of sociology as scholarship and as a form of independent criticism essential to social progress. To be sure, there is a technical problem in reconciling this position with the accepted view that sociology cannot be value-free. The role form and its content appear not to fit too well, but the major method of reconciling the two is to treat the value-neutrality of sociological knowledge as a road to be travelled rather than a destination already arrived at. The job of sociologists/intellectuals is seen to be to strive for maximum objectivity and to stress the distance between their judgmental position and the subject-matter being judged.

The second, marxist, view of intellectuals also provides a role for the sociologist as a partisan theorist and committed critic. Here knowledge is produced for a revolutionary class, or in a weak version of this stance is produced to demystify and dehegemonize the ideologies of the powerful. This position ties in well with the character of sociological knowledge as inevitably value-committed. In fact what happens here is that the inevitable epistemological character is traded upon to give form to the role, rather than the reverse as in the Mannheimian version of the intellectuals.

It is clearly understood why intellectuals find themselves in one of these roles. There are few others. If we can accept the pressure towards the role of intellectual we should trade upon it deliberately and capitalize upon the detachment of academic sociology from professionalism and administration. What I am suggesting is that it is the very institutional detachment of sociology which provides its greatest opportunity. This is not an absolute matter of course, it is one of degree. To the degree that academic sociology is institutionally disconnected and can exploit its intellectual autonomy, to that degree it can contribute to social intervention. To that degree its theoretical component can help to illuminate the social problems which are themselves constitutive of all social inquiry.

3 Law and social theory

Why theorize?

Organized societies are by definition constraining on individual and collective freedoms. The only transcendence of this necessary and inevitable constraint is by understanding its character and attempting to justify its promotion or change. This cannot be stressed too highly. As Rex has said, truth is not gained through uninstructed practice or experience,[1] and we might add that attempts to overcome inevitable circumstances by blind or hysterical reaction tragically fail.[2] The founding fathers of sociology attempted in a variety of methodological styles to specify the nature of social constraints in so far as they took the problem of social order (that is, how is society possible?) to be constitutive of social science. The foundations of the sociological study of society rest upon a particular kind of knowledge.

It is faintly embarrassing to talk of the liberative potential of theory, possibly because this could appear to mean the illusory liberation of the imagination only, that is, in a collective sense, the liberation of false consciousness. This is the accusation of the critics of 'bourgeois' social science.[3] As a wholesale condemnation of theoretical work this is as absurd as the blanket criticisms of the value of 'interpretive' sociology which often come from the same source.[4] This issue has been approached already in the first two chapters. The result is, surely, that the proof of the theory pudding is in the eating of the liberative or repressive results.

In this chapter a major set of constraining institutions, practices and knowledges is examined in order to describe the crude benefits that sociology has yielded.

Law is a major sector of social control. It is an imperialistic system of rules which is highly articulate and prone to reification,[5] and which is backed up, in the final resort, by state-authorized coercion and violence. The form of law which we will be considering, that in contemporary western society, is not universal, and the protracted debates about whether or not all societies exhibit the same form of social control[6] or whether there are a series of stages of forms of social control of which law is a late example[7] will not be dealt with here. It does seem as if there are analytic levels of the conception of law as a theoretical object — for instance law in general, idealized epochal law and particular historically located forms of law — which it would be a mistake to confuse or ignore. But the initial focus here is on contemporary English law, especially criminal law, and only secondarily on the other two levels. Law is a remarkably deep-laid and fateful set of institutions and practices based upon and giving rise to forms of knowledge — doctrines, principles and actual laws themselves — which have been for a very long time impervious to sociological examination. In a literal sense law is canonical.

In part this status of law rests upon the plausibility with which it has itself prohibited, by argument, its own description and criticism. The most striking example of this is the assumption of *legalism*.[8] This is the ideology of the deliberate isolation of the legal system as some sort of neutral social entity which is at once the guarantee and expression of man's preference for order over chaos in society; the belief that law is society's only protection against a war of all against all. As a basic belief few would challenge its commonsense relevance. But to the extent that the *sui generis* quality of social control is imported as a justification of particular forms of law and legal system it becomes an obstacle to sociological rationality. To a great extent lawyers have been guilty of serving the 'church' and not the 'divinity' in that even the most sociologically and theoretically sophisticated lawyers start from an assumption of the necessity of legalism.

There are, very broadly, two areas which lawyers have neglected to examine and in the neglect have reified. The first is the operational character of the legal system: who has power over what outcomes; who benefits and who suffers; what are the intended and unintended consequences; what are the connections between the legal system and other institutional parts of the society? Those lawyers and legal administrators who have been concerned with reforming the legal system have largely waited for scandal, exposure or popular protest to push them towards change. It is arguable that journalism has been more concerned to monitor the actual workings of the law than lawyers themselves.

Yet, given the vested interests of lawyers in the inviolability of law, they have not been well served by sociologists, part of whose job has come to be the observation of the parts of society's institutional structure from a functional viewpoint and whose research position within the organization of the state allows it a degree of independence. It is not the intention here to enter the unresolvable argument about whether sociologists should engage in a sociology *for* or a sociology *of* law.[9] In any case there seems to be no real reason to suppose a long-term conflict of the approaches as significantly possible, though in the short term the conflict is a useful and clarifying one. Sociologists are increasingly committed to examining how the law works on a day-to-day and a historical basis.

The other area concerns the knowledge upon which our law is based, its status as knowledge and how it has changed. Unlike many other institutional sectors of society knowledge in the legal system is for lawyers themselves the dramatic *fons et origo* of their activity. Their knowledge in the form of written laws and written judgments is their only basic resource. All expertise and authority is related to the intrinsic importance of their unmediated knowledge. Although in fact much court-room work had been shown to rest on tacit and unexplicated assumptions and rules of thumb,[10] recourse is necessarily made to knowledge in law books as the unarguable and unquestionable foundation of their power and their excuse for authority. This peculiar status and vulnerability of professional knowledge is recognized by lawyers in at least one revealing way. Through the medium of jurisprudence lawyers have themselves colonized all the authorized rights of commentary on and elaboration of legal knowledge. Although in fact much court-room work has been theoretical work can be carried on[11] and it has been monopolized by lawyers. It is in this area that sociological theory can be revealing, helpful and truly reformative.

Jurisprudence

Jurisprudence as an area of study and research for lawyers (mainly academic lawyers) is not a subject with a coherent theoretical object and is not unified by a methodology or a clear educational purpose. For some time it has been realized that this area of legal knowledge has a confused and chaotic content,[12] the history of which is a succession of attempts to impose a theoretical foundation or at least a purpose.[13] The history of jurisprudence as a 'subject' or part of a discipline can be revealing provided it is not viewed as a simple history of ideas in which a lurching and uneven transition is made between historicism, positivism, formalism and realism as the guiding beliefs. At any rate it has been the academic repository of lawyers' theory and more lawyers have now come to realize that its theoretical underdevelopment may help to explain the very character of law, while jurisprudence as taught to lawyers comes to act as the camouflage for legal peculiarity.[14]

Much of the fear of the explicit consideration of jurisprudence as an insecure form of legal theory can be seen in the attempts to define jurisprudence in such a formal or idiosyncratic way that sociological theorizing is excluded by definition. For instance, the stress often put upon the formally analytical character of jurisprudence such that it becomes a 'focus on facilitating our vision of the logical coherence of the several propositions and parts of a legal order and on fixing the definitions of terms used, and the presuppositions which will maximise such coherence'.[15] The emphasis on logic in the syllogistic sense,[16] on fundamental *sui generis* legal relations,[17] or on basic irreducible norms,[18] are exercises in 'the systematic dogmatisation of a peculiar system of law'.[19] That is, they are attempts to elevate the status of legal knowledge to a height beyond the reach of conventional theoretical discussion. They try to formalize the discussion of legal theory in such a way as to render it devoid of substantive content.[20] As we have noted previously, this is a common development in the self-consciously theoretical parts of disciplines. But in a discipline which owes it existence to a practice imbued with such fateful and immediate consequences for everyday life this formalizing habit functions very conservatively. As Campbell notes,[21] a legal scheme is an interpretation of reality based on a model used by practical lawyers and judges whose basic constraint is the necessity of decision. Campbell states that the world view of jurisprudence is one of pragmatic and practical problem-solving,[22] and that theory in this case is attached to the maintenance of the rules and indeed their reification. Thus the rationality of law which, it is claimed, is based on logic is, in fact, like all social rationality culturally relative.

Increasingly more sceptical studies of what jurisprudence has taken for granted are available from lawyers themselves. For instance Eckhoff and Sundby's study of the character of the so-called 'basic norms' and their explanation of how a process of circular reasoning is implicitly accepted which equates 'basic' with 'internalized' is a model of lawyers' own scepticism about jurisprudence.[23] But lawyers also look towards sociology for some contribution to understanding the status of their own knowledge, though sometimes with some pessimism.[24] Schiff calls for a 'new jurisprudence' which starts with the question 'what is society?' rather than 'what is law?'.[25]

In spite of the earlier call for a substantive rather than formal theory of law this does not mean persistently confusing abstract concepts and empirical observations.[26] It means examining jurisprudence from a sociology of knowledge perspective.[27] Jurists out of the nature of their specific practice always imagine that they are dealing with *a priori* principle[28] and have invented a form of theory to reinforce this untenable assumption, untenable, that is, unless we revert to a conception of natural or divine law. The search for essential meanings of law[29] is an inappropriate task for jurisprudence and will provide only utopian frames of reference.

What then might law ask of jurisprudence? Perhaps we should separate what have been called the educational or therapeutic functions[30] from the directing functions jurisprudence serves in

41

law-making and enforcement, and the rationalizing functions it performs for legal change. It is that part of the division of legal labour which can provide general theories which act as reasons for and explanations of the way law as a whole operates in society. The enormous disciplinary eclecticism which underlies jurisprudence has up to now resulted in the lack of any focus, and this very variety of 'relevant' areas has been used to fend off the central relevance of a sociological theory of law and to embrace philosophy as some kind of immediately obvious theoretical basis[31] or history, again as the obviously important explanatory 'story' of law.[32] Techniques of conceptual analysis, discussions of principle and charts of changes in legal codes are important, but as the major components of a discipline they can provide no answers to questions which must arise prior to them, namely questions about the connection between law and society and about how theories of society will direct inquiry to particular kinds of relations.

What law might ask of sociology

There seems little obvious practical reason why any professional or vocational group should require the services of sociologists interested in theory. Lawyers appear to be pragmatic and problem-oriented. Yet like most groups united only by the *rites de passage* of their professional protective body they are a loose coalition of a wide range of jobs, including not only pleading and arguing but advising a range of individuals and groups, teaching, researching and theorizing about law as an intrinsically interesting and worthwhile activity. In the short term social theory will help and enlighten only some of these practitioners. In the long term it can benefit all. Yet lawyers' definitions of legal problems, and more pertinently social problems, are such as to make recourse to any of the social disciplines seem irrelevant. There is an incompatibility between legal and sociological reasoning[33] which is one of the conditions for this, though not everybody agrees on the strength of the conflict.[34] Some lawyers will ask of the social disciplines only for that which they think will make them more efficient in the terms prescribed by legal practice itself. Much of the concern with the relations between particular social changes and law have this 'efficiency' as their inspiration.[35] Their definitions of social problems will be confined to those areas of 'trouble' in our society that the law can affect *other things remaining equal.* The *ceteris paribus* assumption among lawyers can be related back to their belief in the law being naturally given and naturally separate from and superior to political agencies.[36] Those lawyers starting with law as the fixed point rather than starting from the idea of society as simply the relationship existing between institutions over time will not welcome any methodology which tries to make relative that which had been the fixed reason for inquiry in the first place.

There is more than a little self-delusion in lawyers' attempts to broaden the law by the use of sociology[37] as though it were a vehicle, like a tram, the speed of which could be regulated but the direction of which was fixed. Sociology and especially social theory is more likely to run down anyone who interferes with the steering and notably those whose vocationalism is the main shaper of their theory. Law, based upon a belief in its own immanence and teleology, is unlikely to be bolstered up by a discipline which aims to demystify, dereify and generally smash all pedestals if not all icons. The likely effect of social theory on lawyers is to impress them with the artificial quality and very partial (in both senses of the word) effects of formal law. Thus it would be unwise to use social theory as the humanistic icing on the educational cake.

What social theory might ask of law

For a very long time the sociology of law has remained undeveloped and this might be taken to be evidence of sociology's inability to handle the area and make sense of its development and social position. In part this may be true but the central position of law for Weber[38] and Durkheim[39] and rather less explicitly for Marx[40] suggests that the sociology of law has lapsed rather than never begun. It seems more likely that law itself has been peculiarly resistant to sociological penetration of virtually any form. The power, prestige and independence of the legal system, themselves increasingly important areas for social science scrutiny, have been sufficient to guarantee an alarming degree of immunity when combined with the aura of fear and mystification which surround the image of law in public opinion.[41] There is also a degree of intrinsic opaqueness and inscrutability to law (which is often exaggerated) and more importantly a status underwritten by the state apparatus which has warned off open sociological research.[42] Sociologists have not found it an attractive area for research.

This is more than a shame. The law is a very obvious point of intersection for the major antinomies which sociologists have revealed as constituting the vital contradictions of all parts of our society. Not only is the law a paradigm example of the mutual reinforcement of power position and social knowledge (or if one prefers of social class and ideology), it is also, when considered as a theoretical object, a nexus of the contradictions between conflict and consensus assumptions of the social order, between individualism and collectivism, between determinism and voluntarism and between description and prescription. This is simply a clumsy way of suggesting that a consideration of law from the point of view of established social theorizing is at least as illuminating as the scrutiny of all other parts of our institutional structure, with the added importance that law has considerably more obvious and describable consequences than many other areas. All parts of society are opaque, and sometimes even invisible to sociologists to some degree, and the coincidence between the official 'charter' of an organization or institution and its actual practices and functions is often tenuous. There are many institutions which function as social control agencies in a hidden way (for instance social work), having a charter of 'aid' or even 'therapy'. Law is an area where the overt charter and actual function appear to coincide in a relatively unusual way. That is, law is one of the few areas, perhaps the only area, where social control is openly acknowledged, practised and publicized. For this reason it is of great interest to sociologists.

The strength with which law asserts its independence and neutrality not only from politics and historical pressures, but also from scrutiny, now makes it a priority for study. The claim of a form of knowledge and practice to autonomy from society is always viewed by all kinds of sociologists with scepticism. Whether it is science, medicine, religion or law sociologists are unwilling to allow these complexes of belief and action an *a priori* supra-social character, and in general the sociology of science, medicine and religion have vindicated the core sociological stance that everything in society is social. The development of these social institutions owes more to the historical accumulation of social pressures and events than it does to some logic intrinsic to the knowledge or practice in question. Insider accounts of these areas always stress the intrinsic logic and by so doing reify their subject. Sociologists have still to demystify law in this sense though there are indications that the process has started. The most obvious relevant indicator which also illustrates the role of social therapy in this dereifying process is the sociology of deviance.

The sociology of deviance

The history of criminology and more especially of the sociological study of deviant behaviour is both an example of and a contribution to the likely natural history of the sociology of law. It is a pertinent case study of the dethronement of canonical notions of crime and the criminal and the inversion of the relation between the theoretical object – crime – and the rule system which so defined it – law. The sociology of deviance has become in large part the sociology of law.

There are many excellent available overviews of the history of criminology,[43] though few deal with the change in theory *and* with the changing theory–practice relationship. But all recent narratives take the development of an interactionist sociology of deviance and latterly of a materialist marxist account of deviance as being major epistemological shifts which have had dramatic academic consequences.

The early history of criminology as a subject, and such early sociology of deviant behaviour as there was, reveals a discipline partially constituted by developing social control agencies of the time, and partly by developments in biology, medicine and philosophy autonomously developing within those disciplines.

45

Histories of British[44] and American[45] criminology have noted the interaction between the demands of the state, both practical and ideological, and the internal impetus of expanding and developing bodies of knowledge. Concentrating on one at the expense of the other provides a distorted picture. The coincidence of state demand and academic focus in early twentieth-century British criminology was such as to create the 'criminal' or at best the 'criminal group' as the unquestioned and obvious analytical object. The domination of a legalist conception of harm and medical and psychiatric notions of deviation on the one hand, and the increasing administrative reach of the state combined with a number of evangelistic ideologies concerning the degree to which the state should be involved in social defence and individual protection on the other, combined to erect and bolster a particularly anti-sociological view of crime and deviant behaviour.

The partial and irrational consequences of the reinforcement/ interaction of institution and ideology in criminology are now well and passionately documented.[46] The ignoring and therefore the excuse of the crimes of the powerful and the denial of the existence of a real scale of social harms by biasing the frame of reference of deviance in this way seems likely to be something from which even a self-consciously radical criminology will be unable to escape.

The most convenient way of grasping the shift in criminology from this position to a new truly sociological view of deviance is to examine what is set out for analysis and what is protected as 'objective' and is unavailable for or is beyond analysis. Conventional criminology took the generation and enforcement of laws as the established basis for examining crime. In a social situation of rule-making and rule-breaking only infraction was seen as a valid object of study. In a sense this shows us a misuse of the word 'study', for it is hard to believe that researchers could at particular moments cut off their subjects, in a theoretical sense, from the changing rule structure. What then was taken for granted in formulating the problems to be investigated was law itself. Backed up by beliefs in natural law and the solemn state-guaranteed authority of legal organization, reflexivity in the sense of the researchers' assessment of their own position in relation to their object of study was irrelevant. The object was constituted by the researchers' position and interest as members of a society, as was the knowledge itself which appeared to give a justification to the boundaries of study.

The involvement of sociology in this kind of criminology is explainable only as a consequence of the lack of a well developed substantive sociological theory tradition. Retrospective accounts of mainstream sociological contributions to criminology[47] organize their narratives in terms of specifically theoretical developments, but this has become the conventional style of sociology's own historiography and there is little evidence to show an independent theoretical development at the time. Indeed the case might be made that functionalist criminology, apparently an obviously independent theoretical development, was in large part a response to societal and state demands for a quasi-scientific and impressively rhetorical *form* of analysis.[48]

The slackening of the force of these demands and the development of an 'anti-utilitarian' culture[49] as an unintended and unforeseen reaction to state activity after the war provided the conditions for the reversal of the explanans and the explanandum of criminology – law and the criminal. It was the jettisoning by sociologists of lawyers' and medical men's faith in the supra-social character of the theoretical objects of their own disciplines (law and a biological view of man), an abandonment of a received ontology, that allowed the prime focus to switch to precisely those areas which had been assumed to be, almost literally, beyond question and certainly beyond incrimination. The initial result was the adoption of the process of meaning construction by the putative deviant as the new analytic object and subsequently of the social conditions and character of rule-making itself.

Already developed general theories, embracing characteristic ontologies and epistemologies, were the mills in which the criminological material was ground fine. Phenomenology and marxism were the already existing forms of analysis which provided the muscle-power. But they pre-existed the developments in criminology. The cultural conditions of the society and of academic sociology changed in such a way that the potentials in these areas were called forth for more general use.

A sociology of deviance which does not fix upon rules and upon particular kinds of rules like law, as a primary referent is facile and retrospective and is at risk of becoming an unquestioning tool of an existing social control apparatus rather than a serious and critical study.

All I am suggesting in this thumb-nail sketch of the sociology of deviance is that it is the change in theoretical object which is the significant marker of disciplinary progress. The extent to which this theoretical change is determined by changing social structural and political conditions and the extent to which it is attributable to real theoretical developments deriving from theoretical work is a major area for discussion. At any rate the practical social effects, especially at the level of policy, are unarguable. At the very least there now exists a rival to the official social control criminologies fostered by the state for its own purposes. The degree of independence gained by a pluralism of theory, questioning the propriety of those very purposes, is to the social good and is the bed-rock for an independent social science. It is uncomfortable that the status of the law-maker and enforcer is equalized in analysis with the rule-breaker, and much of the resistance to such change may be attributable to the sense of a yawning practical chasm opening at our feet.[50] But, once arrived at, a theoretical object cannot be ignored or side-stepped, it can only be progressively overcome by its replacement in theory.

The two areas most dramatically mystified by law are also two issues fundamental to sociological theory in general; the assumption of a conflict or consensus view of social order and the assumption of an individualist or collectivist basis for both understanding society and for organizing its social control. Both of these areas are about the plausibility of certain assumptions crucial to the whole direction of law and legal reform and central to our orientation towards the inevitable character of our society. Each area is illuminated by sociological theory already familiar to sociologists.

Conflict and consensus

The belief that society is at root and by nature a co-operative system in which fundamentals are shared by all, and that violence and coercion are only pathological or superficial, or that society is basically an enforced truce, domination or perhaps fragile misconception or mystification, is constitutive of social thought. It cannot be stressed too highly that these are mutually incompatible views which are inevitable assumptions made by all people and more pertinently by all policy-makers and social control agencies. While we may see a mixture of conflict and consensus around us in the forms of the reproduction of social life we cannot adopt a 'mixed' theory of the historical patterns of their empirical variation.[51] The choice between a conflict or a consensus account of society is a major constraining choice on our research and practice and although it is often seen as a crude distinction it is the major initial choice to be made.

To summarize the two gross positions briefly we might say that a consensus view of society sees no basic conflicts in society either of interest or belief. Society is largely in equilibrium and is largely efficient in rewarding interaction and effort. At root society rests upon some sort of central value system which has an historical character and a set of institutional supports. This wide value consensus sets the outer limits of society's identity and it is within these that sectional disagreements, mistakes, accidents, deviance and generally what appears to be conflict takes place. Such apparent conflicts may even be necessary for the wider consensus. The fact that society simply *is* or continues to *be* is the ultimate vindication of such beliefs. Plainly the accent on the, within narrow limits, variable character of the satisfactory functioning of institutions allows a range of very visible conflicts (stretching from collective bargaining to rebellion) to be accounted for without denying the ultimate consensual framework. One of the best examples of such consensus theory in operation is in the liberal account of the constitutional basis of the British state.[52] There we have a description of a system of 'checks and balances' with an overall benevolent purpose which forms the machinery for the operation of consensus; that is the organization of representation and decision-making, and enforcement is the apparatus which mirrors the natural diversity of needs within a wider identity of interests.

A conflict approach begins from an assumption of scarce resources and constraint as the natural character of society. A variety of final reasons may be used to account for this and there are a number of different kinds of conflict theory which may locate essential conflict in human nature, the market or in production itself.[53] All conflict theories describe society as a zero-sum game in which institutions and rules are attempts by those who gain physical power to maintain their control over the inherently centripetal forces of society. Thus whereas under the aegis of a consensus approach social arrangements may take on the character of the reflection of a natural order, especially of a natural hierarchy, and thus are justified by their natural character, under a conflict perspective such historically specific forms are reflections only of the needs of those who dominate (plus the by now mystified beliefs of the dominated).

Is this a stark choice to be faced by all interventionist practices which are founded on social disciplines? Interventionist disciplines like law are, following a conflict theory, themselves embedded in the inevitable domination of society and thus should not be expected to embody in their knowledge and theory the seeds of their own destruction or at best their relativizing. Apart from self-confessed absolutist and authoritarian regimes the institutions of social control are unlikely to justify their operations and character as anything other than consensus-based.

Until recently those social theorists who have been concerned to contribute to legal theory have been dominated by consensualism.[54] Parsons, one of the most detailed and monumental of consensus theorists of contemporary sociology, is concerned to show how official norms represent society's own highest values and that law takes its place with other 'natural' agencies such as socialization as the inevitable form of the integration and reintegration of behaviour into the social equilibrium.[55] Sorokin[56] or Timasheff[57] similarly attempt to reason a three-way correspondence between society's 'ethical mentality' as a whole, its law and its power structure, and

Timasheff tried to describe the natural evolutionary development of this. The *locus classicus* of a consensus approach to law in society is Durkheim's work on law as an expression of the *conscience collective*.[58]

All these theorists see a natural consensus in society. The use of power is assumed to be in the long term reflective of or immaterial to a fundamental cohesiveness and is thus given low priority as an important analytical focus. What are the implications of such a set of assumptions for law's self-consciousness?

The law holds itself to be a value-neutral framework in which inevitable but essentially socially superficial individual and sectional conflict can be peacefully resolved by an appeal to a set of agreed social values. At the least, even if there is a high degree of pluralism in society and some public contention about social values, the law is the only arena for the resolution of such conflicts.[59] The law sees itself as removed constitutionally and actually from the visible ruck and justifies the neutrality of law by an appeal to some 'universe of pre-existing cognoscible forms',[60] by a resort to metaphysics or by the belief that law cannot but follow on from custom, folkways or deep norms; that is, law's very survival and flourishing is evidence of its high degree of fit with a shared culture. Within this broad platform supporting law's prestige as a form of social control there are a variety of positions: utilitarians and social contract theorists holding certain views on all individuals' agreement with the desirability of private property and welfare, sociologically more sophisticated legal theorists reading off an evolution of legal forms and statuses connectedly with societal evolution, liberal pluralists who recognize lag and phase problems of legal and wider cultural change but who see in law's procedural rules a solid rock-bottom of agreement.

For the conflict theorist even apparent harmony and consensus is an example of misperception, false-consciousness and manipulation. Once penetrated, analytically, this crust of cohesion will reveal the authentic level of actual consensus. This is important in that simply specifying conflict as the fundament of social life will allow a variety of characteristics of that conflict.

The analytic question is – is the conflict patterned and how is that pattern to be understood if it exists? As Binns has shown,[61] there is a profound difference between locating conflict at the level of market interaction, that is distribution, as he suggests Weber does, and at the level of production by the appropriation of surplus value which then explains 'the social reproduction of structured class antagonisms',[62] as Marx does. The citation of Marx as the source of conflict theory is no longer helpful if we are concerned with locating the point at which change will bring about a possibility of a wider consensus and if we wish to eschew utopianism.

Increasingly social scientists concerned with the law have become interested in some form of conflict theory. It is the rise of conflict theory, and especially Marx-inspired conflict theory, which accounts for the existence of a sceptical sociology of law. The law is seen as a method by which those in power maintain their position. This can be viewed as an almost visible conspiracy of élites[63] or as a subtle and complicated historical process.[64] The question of which social group's interests are embodied in law and how these interests are mediated either actually in law-making and enforcement or ideologically in the public's perception of law is a complex area for research, the pursuit of which would quite legitimately collapse an empirical sociology of law into the sociology of the state in general. Avoiding such complications for the moment we can say that the law is the method of making state power manifest by creating an effective profile of the punishable and a scale of deviance and normality by the use of punishment. The law is an historical accretion. It reflects in a cumulative though not obviously linear way the ascendancy of particular groups at particular times. This ascendancy and fall must itself be explained to make sense of the law and it is in this way that an initial conflict approach to law requires that we explain much more than the law by reference to some specific sociological theory of historical change such as Marx's or Weber's. Ultimately we assume that the law protects interests, both material and ideological. The complication is that law itself over time creates a morality and an ideology which reifies its own moral choices and the end result is that law creates its own closure to criticism except within rigid limits. It becomes very difficult to question certain assumptions held by law (for instance the issue of the rightness of the rule of law) because they become fixed into the wider culture. It is much more difficult to use a conflict sociology of law than a consensus version and there are fewer well known exponents.

The work of Marx and Engels is the conventional starting-point,[65] with their general theory of the state in which the law is an ideological form which appears to develop an autonomy from material conditions and from the state. There are a few what might be called post-classical marxist approaches to law, the most important of which is Renner's examination of the legal institution of private property[66] and of how the development of private law favoured one group over another in the development of capitalism. The most dramatic development, however, has been the recent interest in law from non-marxist conflict theorists which was inspired in great measure by the increasing interest in crime and deviance as a field of study for sociologists. The basic outlines of this development have already been mentioned and the historical studies of the passing and enforcement of particular laws — especially in the crimes-without-victims category — are well known.[67] To go beyond description such studies had to have a theoretical basis which could explain why and how laws, which themselves created criminal categories, and in a fundamental sense created crime, responded to particular pressure groups in their making and use. Increasingly such studies have become the historiography and sociography of thoroughgoing conflict theories of law which in turn have fed back on to various kinds of conflict theory more libertarian and anarchist than marxist.

For sociologists a conflict approach to law is now becoming the major informing perspective[68] though the variety of overarching theories of the state permitted in this perspective should be stressed.

Plainly this kind of theoretical choice and the research work which follows from it have little impact on lawyers' prescribed practices except in so far as this work is one of the influences on lawyers adopting unconventional professional positions. There is certainly the danger that apprentice lawyers will be alienated by such work. It does not aid a smooth, professional career and it does not service the professional self-images so essential to successful legal work. Lawyers, much more than many other occupations which have less colleague control and historically a more insecure status, are immune to new understandings of their parent institution's place in society. The acceptable sociological input is one in which a gloss of information and 'social context' can be brushed on to an otherwise uncriticized institution.[69] There is no obvious and compelling reason why we should accept this. The message of a conflict sociology of law is not to do away with law or to magic lawyers into a utopianist or revolutionary stance.[70] It is merely to make what was previously regarded as obvious and unquestionable open to discussion, and to provide an understanding of our legal apparatus in terms of the society which is both its cause and its consequence. The real impact of such sociological insight, once accepted as a fruitful and sensible form of analysis, is to help the lawyer realize that the degree of independence that the law might realize could be greater than it now is. Without wishing to broach an analysis of how far a sub-system of society can transcend the wider system of which it is a part, we can assume that there is some degree of freedom intrinsic to the knowledge that social theorists can provide for interventionist occupations and that all and any of such inputs can have some effect. The legal profession is more resistant than nearly all others (except perhaps medicine) to such inputs.

If some commentators are correct in their analyses the events which vindicate a conflict theory of society will overtake lawyers, possibly even before they have accepted such accounts. Winkler describes a developing 'corporate state' in which the role of law as the major final means of organization and control of both organizational and individual behaviour will be lessened as other forms of corporate agreement and planning with the state apparatus become popular.[71] That is, other forms of the official regulation of conduct will serve the existing or developing élites better and the formal panoply of law will become a hindrance. Law, like many other professions, is licensed by the state but with a high degree of autonomy. This independence is not sacrosanct or unchangeable and a conflict approach to law points to this and gives an implicit warning. The understanding of law provided by a conflict perspective for law's clients in the form of the illumination of the previously apparently random or unfathomable functions of law must also be appropriate for the practitioners.

Individualism and collectivism

The lessons of sociological theorizing are not the firm conclusions sometimes adopted by writers at the ends of their books but are the issues which are raised and refined in theorists' arguments with each other and each others' ghosts. The continual readdressing of issues over the decades and societies shows us basic, unresolved but pressing alternatives in the social thought of all of us. Conflict and consensus is one such unresolved antinomy. Another major one is the issue of the connection, in principle between the individual and society[72] or, put more crudely and synoptically, between individualism and collectivism. Sociology in its most formative period in Europe between about 1880 and 1920 was preoccupied with this issue, along with other connected problems, and the lack of resolution and even progress constitutes much of contemporary sociological concern. Legal practice and knowledge is founded upon a rhetorical individualism in theory which turns out, in practice, to be an unexplicated, obscure and irrational kind of collectivism. Legal self-consciousness needs at least the open discussion of this issue but persistently confuses it, notably in its own discussion of justice.[73]

Initially we need to distinguish two debates about individuals and collectivities as social units – the analytical (or methodological) and the ethical. First, as a normative principle individualism has obvious ethical resonances. Both Weber[74] and Durkheim[75] were preoccupied with the development of society and its impact on the sensibility of the individual. Weber's discussion of bureaucratic rationality and its crippling effect on the personality was ambiguous in its stance; Durkheim, however, confronted the issue head on and he saw in the change in the collective conscience towards the 'organic' a paradoxical increase in respect for individual rights as the division of labour increased. He was concerned to locate a social discipline which was concerned with social facts, *sui generis* facts which preceded individuals and yet which were only apprehendable in individual acts. Increasingly as the social disciplines become part of the engineering and control of whole societies[76] the value of the individual as the standard of judgment of knowledge and practice becomes contentious. The primacy of the individual and the belief in his moral superiority has come under attack from the scientistic aspirations of the social disciplines which criticize such issues as essentially non-analytic. The response has been an uncritical collectivism on the one hand and a physiological reductionism on the other. A series of widely ramifying philosophical debates which have been as much concerned with the issues of voluntarism and determinism as anything else, have ensued, as well as political debates about the death of liberalism and the organization and extent of state intervention. As O'Neill notes,[77] the crux of the normative issue is the location of power in a historical situation where individuals have become increasingly subject to totalitarian states. Individualists like Popper[78] and Hayek[79] see the irrational crushing of individual autonomy under the state and organizational power. Ironically many writers at the opposite political pole from Hayek and Popper have also been concerned with the problems of an individuality seen in terms both of sensibility and self-determination which is crushed by collective planning and control.

But for most sociologists the ethical issue is at least publicly separate from the methodological issue. This latter refers to the problem of priority in explanation and the ontological status of social and individual entities. Sociology as a discipline is founded on Durkheim's insistence that social facts are *sui generis* and are to be explained only by other social facts, and that the explanation of social by individual facts is methodologically wrong. The subsequent concentration on social institutions and organizations which are collectivities, and systems of rules and resources which are impersonal and which can be called 'structures',[80] has continually provoked difficulty about how changes in collectivities are to be explained. This has often resulted in attempts to telescope the study of collective social phenomena into either history or psychology[81] and thus dispense with sociology as an autonomous discipline.

Hayek holds that real social order is spontaneous and self-generating and if we attempt to make or organize it we depend only on the limits of the individual mind which can direct such organization. Given that knowledge cannot be perfect our tendency to treat 'wholes' as definitely given objects mistakes model constructions and provisional theories for natural units. It is only social science and more especially social scientists which constitute such wholes. Writing frequently and over a long period of time Hayek tries to show that the 'constructivist rationalist' attitude which assumes that all institutions ought to be the product of deliberate design is irrational in the face of the unknown and unknowable. There is a metaphysical centre to Hayek's work which is concerned with human submission to rules which can neither be designed nor ever fully apprehended, but which can still be honoured in action.

Popper's view is that the analytic use of type concepts, for instance in Marx's methodology, is a mistake also, and one which began with Plato. The belief that the state is more real than the individual is wrong, but so also is the psychologism of J. S. Mill in his appeal to human nature as the resting-place of explanation. Popper sees methodological individualism as the only criterion of the satisfactory explanation of social laws. Social systems are not analogous to physical systems and it is the major error of scientism to suppose that social structures or systems have a real as opposed to an analytical identity.

The debate at a methodological level is complex and resolves into one not just of compared epistemologies but of ontologies also. The fact that the level of the individual and of face-to-face interaction has an unavoidable immediacy for all of us might easily push the argument to a crude resolution at the level of socio-biography. Individualism and collectivism as prevailing modes of analysis at different times have their own historical and institutional preconditions.[82] This is not a resolved issue but one which lays out the major choices to be made.

The law as a form of knowledge and practice is heavily and

publicly individualist. Its basic unit is the individual, and certain qualities, important for law, are assumed to inhere in him or her. This may involve obscured reductionist accounts of social behaviour and this is most evident in the *mens rea* rules. The closest the law comes to recognizing a collective fact is in the concept of 'the reasonable man' when a cultural consensus superior to any individual is assumed though the contents of this world view are not schematized. Legal writing fails to examine the idea of social facts and real collective entities and proceeds to treat its subjects as coterminous and concomitant with its subject-matter. That is, the law is assumed to be about people within a society which is itself seen as a purely constitutionally defined and therefore synthetic entity. Collectives such as social classes or even social structures as such which are defined as objects of study and practice constituted by a theory are disallowed. The belief is that individuals as objects of practice and study are unconstituted by a theory and in some sense natural and real. This would only be true in 'natural' interaction, for the status and meaning of individuals in the courts has been theorized by that same law and is distinctly and formally 'unnatural'. In this sense law rests upon a theory of what individuals are, the most striking feature of which is the denial of their membership of collectives or their place in social structures.

The most open theorist of this position is the major anti-collectivist in social science, Hayek himself.[83] Rules of 'just conduct' are derived from a condition of spontaneous order and are discovered.[84] Hayek holds to a conception of natural law which itself specifies the uncollectivized individual as the natural object of reason and practice. This atomistic theory of social organization, while it assumes the priority of the individual, also postulates his imperfectness and requires that he submit himself to conventions and conform to norms which may be laws. A large part of the thrust of Hayek's argument lies in reconstructing a negative view of freedom from government intervention and coercion in order to allow the spontaneous social order to form. To confuse rules of just conduct with rules about the direction and organization of government apparatus both subsumed under 'law' is to confuse individualism and collectivism.

One of the most central ideological areas of law, the concern with justice, is the point where individualist assumptions are most apparent. The recent work of Rawls is a good example.[85] Much of the criticism of his formulation of the liberal theory of justice has highlighted his assumption of methodological and moral individualism.[86] Rawls's view is that the individual is isolated by nature and the principles of justice are about deciding on matters of individual self-interest. The state and its legal machinery operate as a check on individual selfishness (which has a natural quality) and this leads Rawls to a revival of social contract theory which itself was pervasively individualist. Man, then, becomes isolated by legal thought from his real condition of group interest. That is, man, for sociologists, is inexplicable without reference to positions he occupies in society and on strictly *a priori* grounds the inevitability of co-ordinated action and mutual interest pre-constitute the notion of individual rather than the other way round. In situations of group rather than individual conflict the liberal principles of justice become choices to reconceive the basis of behaviour, that is, they are a theoretical choice which is open to great criticism. Such arguments have been put less tendentiously elsewhere.[87]

The principles of individualism and collectivism are central to a critical understanding of the basis of legal social control. Put crudely the law treats collectivities as fictions and members of collectives as isolated individuals which are social products mixed with natural impulses. Complaints about 'class justice' are simply descriptions of the way in which collectives are actually dealt with (because they cannot be avoided in practice) by the law under the ideological camouflage of individualism.

59

4 Social work and social theory

Like 'the law' 'social work' has an immediate reference in our everyday language which the task of sociology is to explore and possibly reconstruct. Just as the law is taken to be, in common sense, the criminal law,[1] so social work is taken to be casework, the face-to-face aiding and supporting relationship between a trained 'expert' and a client who is in some sense officially in trouble. Public and popular images are often accurate as representations of core functions or practices of a job. A case could be made out for penal sanctions being the coercive foundation of law, and similarly for casework as the one distinctive and limiting practice of social work. Even 'radical' writers admit that the occupation is defined traditionally by casework as the professionally supported form of social intervention.[2]

At the moment this traditional and popular conception is under siege from a variety of sociologically inspired positions which would wish to extend the form of intervention. That is, they would wish to recreate what social work practice can be seen to be. Social work is an institution which permits and prescribes a range of practices with a variety of practical objects,[3] which displays an increasing concern with theory and with the choice of theoretical objects in order to feed its practices. The state of flux in social work as a profession[4] and the increasing demands made upon social work by the state[5] render it a form of established social intervention (like law) which is increasingly open to education by theoretical argument (unlike law).

In order to side-step contemporary controversies about what the practice of social work should be, which might properly be the subject of discussion rather than its limitation, it is possible to focus upon social work as an institution which has a history and which interacts with other institutions in society. No analysis of history and interaction can be carried on without a directing theory. That is, no *basic* definition of social work practices is possible beyond the anodyne or the tautological without explicit selection of a theory and a theoretical object. But we can choose a relatively unproblematic level of analysis to begin with. The level of *institution* locates social work as a relatively well embedded set of social relationships, an apparatus, an organization, a personnel and a body of knowledge which exists though it may change over time.

Welfare

This institution is ostensibly concerned with welfare. This is a term which needs explaining. Welfare is not a specific task performed by all societies with a wide variety of methods and rules as, for instance, education or even, arguably, law can be conceived to be. It has a limited and historically located meaning. It refers to state interventions which began at the very end of the sixteenth century with the Poor Laws. There is no timeless or purely human quality about 'welfare'. It is a social product. According to Jordan[6] two major conceptions of welfare have ever since competed for supremacy: that conception holding to belief in the welfare of society as a whole and as a collective unit in which the welfare of particular strategically placed groups or individuals is of secondary interest; and that conception rooted in the belief in the ineradicable incapability of one particular section of society, the poor, over whom paternalistic control could be rightly and morally exercised. Residually there is a third conception which sees welfare as concerned with the standard of living of all citizens, not conceived as aggregated into a social whole. The alternation between such conceptions of welfare and the subsequent changing character of the welfare institution attest to the importance of theories of welfare. Welfare has a structural place in our society which it is hard to see being eliminated but it has a changing meaning and thus a changing knowledge base.

Within all the conceptions of welfare there are a variety of levels of practice from policy-making and political activity through advocacy and group organization to individual casework. The limitation to casework alone within the institution of welfare is a result of the response of the division of labour in society to political, moral and academic pressures. The treatment of welfare as social work defined in limited casework terms would be a dangerous limitation comparable to the definition of medicine as doctoring. Social work like many professionalizing occupations is now experiencing internal pressures to realign accepted and licensed practice with a more basic understanding of the place of the institution itself, and this may be directly attributable to the impact of social science scrutiny. An understanding of ideologies of welfare and of the structural position of the welfare institution is prior to a consideration of the use of social theories by social workers.

What we seem to be faced with is variability and dissensus in the definition of social work and welfare. At the very least we see commonsense views of social work, social workers' own self-consciousness, sociologists' views, and a variety of political and administrative perspectives with various historical pedigrees. Debate about what social work is seems greater and more disorganized than in many other analytically comparable areas of social intervention. For the purposes of discussion we seem to need to search for some core practice and theory and many social-work writers cling to the casework conception as the only available life raft in a tempest of disagreement. Casework *is* social work to many writers because this is demonstrably what most licensed social workers can be seen to do. This sort of definition allocates to practice only what is obvious. After all, casework may actually have an overall social function which is not obvious at all. Other writers[7] deliberately choose some kind of commonsense pre-sociological core which they see as human rather than social. In a field where all explicit theories of practice are borrowed from other disciplines[8] and where there is no organized theoretical commitment or activity, theory itself is a poor basis for defining core attributes, and practice itself seems to speak to the issue alone. Practice looks obvious and controllable and the state as the agency of political and administrative control is presumably concerned to maximize its authority by defining professions as pure practices, the theories and knowledge bases of which are ephemeral or residual. So long as professional practice can be controlled directly as an employee or indirectly as a sort of licensee, and so long as this control is threatened by no more than wage revolts, ideas, theories and ideologies will seem irrelevant. This is because an idea inspiring an inconvenient practice (for instance self-treatment, de-schooling, or direct participation) can be dealt with easily at the level of practice.

The collusion between professions and the state to protect privileged or convenient practices is an interesting area for study and is basic to the understanding of changing social intervention. Social workers, unlike lawyers or doctors, the established professions, are at a stage of theoretical consciousness which when combined with low rewards for relinquishing the control of practice render them like teachers or town planners, more open to theories about practice.

The disciplinary basis of social work

Forms of organized social intervention do not grow naturally out of developments in knowledge. The commitment to intervention and the basis for its organization derives from the political and moral requirement to control and intervene which itself results from the development of society's hierarchy and division of labour. The impetus is social. Knowledge and its organized and institutional forms − disciplines − is called forth by this pre-existing demand. This is true for all forms of organized social intervention. Yet the relationship between 'external' demands and the 'internal' provocation of disciplinary developments is plainly powerful enough to generate contradictions in, or at least difficulties for, the hierarchical division of labour in professions.[9] But in social work there has been no such disciplinary generator and professional practice has been dramatically parasitic upon other disciplines for at least its thetorical knowledge base. This is not to deny that all interventionist practices feed off the development of ideas in general and seek intellectual nourishment, support and direction where they can find it. But the science-based practices, especially medicine and engineering, have organized and largely controlled their own knowledge production. The social-science-based practices have not.

The history of social work in Britain and the USA is the history of the relationships between on the one hand changing practices, changing theories and an attempted professionalization, and on the other between all these items together, viewed as a disciplinary complex and the changing demands coming from society. As has already been suggested, no definitive account can reveal what actually happened. A theoretically chosen account can simply be seen as making understandable what was previously regarded as incomprehensible or contradictory. The more narrowly the problem is defined the less difficulty there will be in putting up with unexplained and intractable phenomena. This is one reason why sociologically informed histories of disciplines are uncomfortable for professions; they make too much information germane to allow a self-serving history to be unquestioned.

Thus the history of social work as the genealogical table of legislation and administrative regulation[10] is merely a description of one area to be explained. All narratives of this kind make problematic what they sometimes pretend to have explained.

The acceptance of social work as an unelaborated and common language occupational description is the acceptance of an object of study which is entirely untheorized. A more sophisticated but still inadequate object would be the constellation of actual practices carried out by social workers. A still more adequate and useful approach would be to describe the central conflicts which the practice of social work now presents to social workers themselves and their 'clients'. The assumption here is that a history of theory and practice addresses the inadequacies of practice as the basic thing to be explained. This does not mean that the inefficiencies of social work are taken as the reason for study, for this would be to accept an administrator's theory alone. It means that conflicts and antagonisms are constitutive of the initial interest that sociology has in a phenomenon. It means that we adopt a conflict theory.[11] We should be clear at this stage that a thoroughgoing theoretical approach would make formal analytical problems themselves the object of study. To the degree to which this is eschewed a primary selection must be made of substantive issues which are then theorized.

An example of a history of social work which seems to adopt this approach is Seed's brief account.[12] Here a variety of conflicts in the development of the social work occupation are described, especially those between social work as an organization and as a movement, and between bureaucratization and professionalization. The developing knowledge base can be seen in interaction with these tensions which are themselves attributable to wider social changes. Against the background of a permanent and ubiquitous private philanthropy the late nineteenth century saw the development of three separable sources of future social work; the charity organization movement, the newly developing field of study of social administration and direct social action. It was the growth of organized training which led to a demand for professionalism and eventually fragmentation. This was all taking place against a background of the changing organization and image of the state. The role of early nineteenth-century philanthropy, says Seed, was to promote an ideal image of universal harmony and social interest. Its credibility rested as much on its symbolic appropriateness as on its practical effectiveness. By the end of the Second World War the role of the state was very different and its new image, of reconciling the individual and the state, was similarly changed. Thus practice and knowledge cannot be treated as free-floating developments within a purely chronologically defined time span. It is illuminating to see the conflict between the range of tasks specified in legislation and a haltingly developed theory of methods (mainly casework theory developed in America) as the basis for the 'discipline' of social work that we now see. The legislation itself was the result of compromises between competing bureaucratic, political and professional interests and resulted in the official definition of objects of practice and thus analysis, the most startling example of which was the 'problem family' of the 1950s and 1960s. Allied to this a high level political withdrawal from a universalist conception of welfare after the war created a series of new jobs for social workers which were thus responses to problems created by this political selection. Social workers found themselves having target groups rather than specific problems dictated to them as well as particular tactics – for instance distributing information and administering means-tested benefits. This is a source of complaint by some social work writers who sense the bureaucratic and political conditions of their own professional status.[13]

The development of casework theory and of 'behavioural science' for social workers[14] takes on a somewhat ironic character against such a background in the British situation. The range of 'models' or theories which have been used in training contexts to identify and even create disciplines with which aspirant social workers can identify,[15] and the fervour with which a systems approach is now being evangelized,[16] can be seen either as camouflage for an increasing manipulation or de-skilling of what identifiable practices have been retained from social work's 'voluntary' era, or as an attempt by a group who sense the impossibility of a status as 'independent' or 'expert' to dredge some authority from an appeal to a knowledge base alone.

Viewed from this position complaints about the 'psychiatric deluge'[17] or the role of sociology in a 'radical' social work[18] become superficial. The espousal of psychoanalytic doctrines as a disciplinary foundation, while it had most impact in USA, has had less effect as a form of theory in Britain, and is puny as a determinant compared with the confident control over permissible practice exercised by the state. The choice of a theory becomes a cosmetic which may well provide rationales for training courses but which can never be more than nostalgic for practitioners faced with statutory mandates and grotesquely expanding case loads.

There is an institutional basis to practice which a social worker must understand before he can state how theory should affect his practice. This institutional basis is revealed by an understanding of how control over practice was historically established, who exercises it, what threats to it exist and what room for discretion the social work practitioner has. The conflict between bureaucratization and professionalization provides the lowest common denominator of such an understanding. The 'discipline' of social work, or its knowledge base, is reactive to its permitted or required practice.

Social work as theoryless practice

Social work has not been concerned with theory or with the philosophy which is parasitic upon theory. In training it has been noticed that students rely on maxims rather than analysis and feelings rather than ideas.[19] At the level of the academic unification of social work in texts and journals this is bolstered by a persistent distrust and dismissal of social science theory. For instance 'to try to build a social work house on the shifting sands of social science theory is asking for trouble. Social work should probably concentrate on erecting strong, portable, flexible tents rather than houses.'[20] Apart from the illogicality of this statement (shifting sands are a sensible reason for having a tent) it illustrates a typical avoidance of theory seen in many social work writers.

Butrym,[21] who holds strongly to the view that theory follows and derives from practice, castigates recent social work for either 'fashion-mongering' or an 'excessive adherence' to one theory, and yet she realizes that social work is vulnerable to the vagaries of practice. Her solution is to substitute a discussion of the place of moral values in general, rather than about choices between incompatible values. This position is a common one. It leads her to state that social work must conceptualize from the experience of practice, but this experience is itself seen as pure and uninterpreted by the social worker's own theory. Self-consciousness by the social worker about the value of individual moral judgment has very little of the reflexive potential that theoretical awareness brings. Theory as such is relegated to generalizations for operational purposes, and the criterion for judging good and bad generalizations is 'goodness of fit'.[22] Butrym treats social work (a 'unique amalgam of instrumental values, applied knowledge, practical skills and specific social context'[23]) as simply a morally inspired but theoryless practice.

Some social work writers are more thoughtful about the relevance of theory. Evans distinguishes between two kinds of knowledge (which he misleadingly calls theory) relevant to social work: the explicit 'theory of practice' derived from social science and the 'practice theory' derived from common sense and work experience.[24] These are seen in some kind of 'dialectical' relationship which means that the origins and implications of any particular theory are avoided by analysis and tested only in 'praxis' which seems to rule out any standards of falsifiability at all. What appears on the surface to be a promising consideration of social work practice's use of theory turns into a circular declaration of the obvious.

Even those writers overtly concerned to demonstrate the relevance of sociology to social work have stressed the overriding relevance of empirical data and the exposé function of sociological research.[25]

Recently the position is typified by Bartlett's attempt to set out a 'common base for social work practice'.[26] In an interesting and prolonged construction of an ideal social work Bartlett acknowledges the view that theory is important[27] and that social work education adopts a method of case study teaching which fosters a dominant anti-intellectualism. But she resorts to a work-task definition which is derived only intuitively ('tasks' and 'coping'). Within the body of conventional reflections on the nature of social work only Smalley overtly adopts the position that practice should grow out of theory,[28] but she calls theory the 'generic principles' of social work. These principles Smalley is clear are not techniques or skills or rules of thumb but neither are they theoretically derived in the sense which we have used so far. They rest on 'understanding',[29] which is again a synonym for intuition.

These positions are all varieties of nods in the direction of recognizing the importance of theory but little more. In social work writing we see a view that initial practice is theory-free and that unmediated and obvious experience is the definer of that practice. Theoretical activity becomes at most a way of justifying existing practice or classifying it for administrative or training purposes. Pleas for the development of social work theory thus have the character of rhetorical bids for professionalism through the almost purely literary inflation of unreflected practices.

Psychiatry and politics as disciplinary bases

At what level of abstraction are we to look for the theory which necessarily guides social work? It might seem sensible to say that the theory is visible not in the directing power it displays over day-to-day practice but that it is seen most clearly in the justifications for shifts or changes in practice. That is, theory is manifested in the combative ideologies of competing paradigms of social work and in the move from one paradigm to another.

'Paradigm' has come to be an over-used and imprecise term in intellectual history,[30] but it has some recent use in social work writing[31] and heuristically refers to a unified complex of assumptions, tasks, theories and methods which has a community of practitioners who form at least a 'school' and generally an entire tradition. In these terms social work's knowledge base can be seen to present a contemporary attempted shift from a paradigm based upon psychiatry as an informing discipline to one based upon politics. Whether or not these disciplinary bases really do provide important determinants of social work is beside the point; they are believed to do so. This means that the acceptability of the speculative schemes and the chosen objects of enquiry of psychiatry have been threatened by a redefinition of tasks and knowledges drawn from an alternative body of theory and practice. Some writers consider that the domination of psychiatry has been overstated.[32] But the increase of politically evangelical social work literature is undeniable and it bases its attraction on an attack on a psychiatry-founded casework definition of social work. Is the choice between psychiatry and politics (or rather political science) the level at which we should situate the foundation of social work practice in theory?

The choice of an individual or a collective object of study and action which is what the choice between psychiatry or politics implies is a theoretical choice. But it is at such a level of generality when applied in the form of a choice between entire disciplines and it is so unreflected upon that theoretical argument about the nature of the proper object of social work is lost. The arguments surrounding the increasing instability of the psychiatric definition of social work and the threats presented to it by the social disciplines is the major basis of theoretical argument in social work's knowledge base.

Part of this is due to the nature of criticism and paradigm shift itself. Bald statements about the domination of social work by psychiatric theories[33] and the necessity to move towards a more politically or socially 'relevant' body of knowledge are really just rhetorical demands. Arguments about the choice of individual or collective objects of study tend to be ignored in favour of pleas which make reference to some obvious resonance in the values of the audience concerning the omissions of a psychiatric view. The tenability of, say, the Freudian view of the individual is not dealt with as a topic in theory by writers who either simply appeal to an alternative dogma or who wish to generate collective action while by-passing the stages of theoretical analysis which will prescribe it.

Psychiatry and politics function as values or more precisely as ideologies justifying positions taken in a contest over the direction of social work practice. They are the identification marks of committed protagonists in a situation of paradigm uncertainty, and as such are seen not as positions which express a viable range of theoretical choices which will be made and which are mutually exclusive. The use of the individual or the politically organized society as a totem is not conducive to a recognition of their positions in marking out the contours of theories which will provide real rationales for practice. A range of pre-packaged disciplinary orientations is not enough to substantiate a view that social work is a practice which is theoretically directed.

The bid to achieve respectability by social work by latching on to an already established body of knowledge and swallowing whole its objects of study and analysis is seen by some writers as both inevitable and an advantage. Butrym sees the core of social work as necessarily borrowing from other disciplines and that this is inevitable because of the range of potentially relevant knowledge.[34] There is an obvious institutional basis for this in that locating social work training in universities made it necessary for the knowledge base to be legitimized in terms of what was already accepted. Social work appeared early on as a practice in search of a theory and the prestige of psychiatry made it an appropriate candidate as well as its ability to unify the object of analysis and the object of practice. But we should note that the choice of psychiatry or politics, or any other university-based discipline like sociology for that matter, is not a theoretical commitment. It is an attempt to adopt a prestigious knowledge base.

Sociology and social work

There have been close and complicated organizational relations between the academic subject of sociology and the training of social workers. Untangling the connections between social work, social studies, social administration and sociology would be a revealing indication of official views of what the theory and practice of social work should be. Due possibly to the administrative connection between sociology and social work in academic institutions it is in many ways surprising that social work practice seems to have had more effect on academic sociology, at least in the British empirical 'blue book' tradition, than the reverse. But the purposeful contribution to social work by sociologists has been increasing over the last ten or so years. Increasingly the contribution reinforces social workers' insecurities about the theoretical basis of their practice. However, in large part the contribution of sociologists has been a-theoretical and been directed towards supplying social workers with at most generalized descriptions of the society and especially those parts of it which it is believed social workers must inhabit. Where theory is presented it is put forward as a series of unconnected 'insights'[35] or models for the purpose of analysis; that is as fresh ways of making sense of the same facts. The contributions of the late 1960s and early 1970s[36] were directed at students and seem to be conceived as timely alternatives to psychiatric and psychological domination. The 'Trojan horse' function which Heraud speaks of was one in which the facts, suitably organized by middle-range theories, spoke for themselves and in fact shouted loudly enough to raise political and moral questions about the propriety of much conventional social work practice. The importance of such theory was, as Heraud says, to help understand the interaction between social workers, their clients and the environment.[37] In fact most sociology was directed at the client and his environment and there is little evidence at that time of a social theorizing which was reflexive enough to provide a commentary on social workers' actual theory and practice, though much energy was spent in battering an isolated psychiatric view then still taken as dominant.

This sort of contribution was typical of sociology's offering to most professional training at the time. At the most sociology was seen as a sort of exposé of hidden deprivation, depravity and privilege, but generally it was taken as a form of survey research for particular purposes. I do not intend to denigrate this activity, least of all in the context of its era of popularity. But as the division of labour in academic sociology has grown more sophisticated we can expect to see an increasing contribution to the elucidation and criticism of professionals' own knowledges and practices and especially social workers' own theories. One of the major objects of analysis might now be social workers' increasing adoption of an explicit form of social theory, the systems approach.

Systems theory

We have seen over the last few years the almost wholesale switch of organized social work from a theoretical eclecticism and muddle, but with a base in developmental psychology, to a kind of social theorizing which has itself been the object of much criticism within sociology. The conditions of this important theoretical election are quite mysterious. Some of the relevant writings[38] cite the publication of particular books in the USA, especially those of Pincus and Minahan[39] and Goldstein[40] as major conceptual breakthroughs. It seems unlikely that this really is a form of theoretical 'discovery' which places traditional social work thought in jeopardy, and we should be wary anyway of attributing such a major change of emphasis to the intrinsic attraction of suddenly available ideas. The adoption of systems theory does not appear to be the culmination of some kind of theoretical drift either. Both Pincus and Minahan and Goldstein situate their 'integrated' approach within particular historical circumstances where new organizations and agencies and new client problems presented apparently new problems of practice. In this country the Seebohm reorganization which grouped social workers into multi-service agencies forced problems in practice, hitherto isolated, into one arena and created above all new managerial problems.[41] I want to suggest that it is the managerial and administrative practice problems above all else which have created a search for a unifying theory and that social workers are acquiescing in an academicization of this essentially bureaucratic issue.

'Systems theory' is really a misnomer. It is really a complicated and elaborate metaphor for describing what seems to be an inevitable way of thinking. There are a number of similar concepts with a high status in the social disciplines, for instance the concept of evolution, and the idea of a 'surface' form representing a 'deep' structure, which seem to be aggravated forms of everyday thought. Initially the systems approach was seen as an archetype for the unification of all science. All phenomena were seen as 'organized' and a search for the basic principles of this organization was believed to yield a fundamental law of nature which in turn would provide an analytic account of all entities, physical, biological, mechanical and social. All phenomena are seen to be systems or sets of phenomena in interaction which in some sense or other exchange information in attempts to self-regulate and stabilize their character. These exchanges can be mapped, modelled and sometimes, given available techniques, be simulated, and thus a new measure of control is available. On the face of it what seems to be a very commonplace view of the world has had enormous impact on the natural and the social sciences in a relatively short period.

The technological yield of systems theory when applied to physical phenomena is well known and the level of resultant control has been high. It may be seen as a major advance in man's power over the physical world, and more especially over his own sometimes unpredictable physical apparatuses – deliberately created yet sometimes difficult to rule. It is the major form of the management of nature and physical entities and there seems little suggestion that the 'theory' of physical systems is in any serious

73

sense 'wrong'. But the transfer from physical to social phenomena is illegitimate[42] to the extent that social phenomena are constituted by the medium of their perception; that is, that the subject-matter of the social disciplines is in a basic and categoric sense created by those disciplines in the process of theory-making and subsequent research. There are no boundaries to social systems and no significances to the exchanges between hypostatized sub-systems beyond those for which agreement can be reached in a community which wishes to use the assumption of a system for some end. This is true, of course, for every case in which a metaphor is the only understanding possible, and it seems likely that the metaphoric is the sole language in which social analysis can take place. To the extent that we wish to describe the social world in terms of sets and sub-sets of what are assumed to be generically the same phenomena and in terms of equilibrium, closure and feedback internal to those sets, then that is what we will find. In a more than banal sense the wish is father to the thought. Social theory is in part a matter of exposing metaphors so that pretensions to an unjustified ontological status will not pass undiscussed.

With respect to social work and the 'unitary' approach, sociological theory contributes a critique of the systems metaphor and identifies its connection with only one kind of practice. The conventional criticism of systems theory – that it assumes consensus and is inherently conservative – are criticisms which may apply to particular applications of the metaphor and I think do apply in the case of Goldstein and Pincus and Minahan. The attempt by Goldstein to build in conflict and instability by declaring the system 'open' rather than 'closed' is to resort to a well-worn device which is tantamount to reducing the systemic character of the system, for it is unclear what an open system is open to unless the system is believed to be an actual empirical entity. External stimuli from the system's environment are simply a residual way of explaining away a major object of interest – social change – while attempting to retain the heuristic use of a metaphor which cannot encompass the object.

How justified is the metaphor as a theoretical means of constructing a 'generic' discipline for an enforced social work?

An answer to this question in terms of the empirical applicability of the system model to the social world of the social worker would be inadequate, because it would force us towards a very open system model with the consequent theoretical vacuity I have just mentioned. The answer must be phrased in terms of a justification for practice or a particular form of practice. Algie makes it clear that a systems approach justifies particular criteria for the management of social services in a situation of 'value pluralism'.[43] Systems theory appears as a device for modelling the administration of a range of practices which are inherently incompatible and unstable, and reducing conflicting interests to a scheme in which decisions about priorities can be made after the rhetorical display of all available alternatives. After defining 'goals', 'missions' and 'objectives', strategies and tactics must be reduced to a reflection of 'community values' or 'the social values implicit in everyday life'. It is the very plurality, confusion and conflict among such values in a social situation of differential interest in the hypostatized system which creates the management problems which a systems approach can be used to smother. A systems approach cannot help a manager or anyone else choose between alternative social values but it can help him cut a path through them. It is a device for the efficient administration of pre-decided practices or ranges of practice. It is not a theory which can deterministically or even dialectically help in the definition of possible practice.

Systems theory has a history of applications in other professions licensed by the state to intervene as a form of social control confused with help. Its mystagogic function in town planning is a case in point, where in the absence of a theory base and in a situation of attempted professionalization the elaboration of a system perspective into a sociologically camouflaged accountancy framework (cost-benefit analysis, p.p.b.s., etc.) provided a new managerial grip on social diversity. Its amenability to quantification and a technical presentation yielded a plausible methodology for making already decided aims practical in a bureaucratic sense and stabilized centralized decision-making. Its ultimate failure in planning is its inability to build in the most significant aspects of social life, value and interest variation, which in the end render the model inefficient. But it has produced organizational dividends and this is what is happening in social work now.

Theoretical overkill

Theories are not solutions to practical problems. The function of sociological theorizing is to lay bare inevitable choices, not to make those choices. The 'discovery' of new theoretical perspectives and their wholesale application to socially relative and often haphazardly grouped bodies of practices creates an entirely spurious unity of practice which in the end defies the ability of the theory to integrate them. In part sociology bears much of the blame for this, for academic sociology suffers little less than social work the tensions of demands that a unity of theory and practice be created and that its existence be justified by producing new control measures. The lurch from one kind of theory to another in sociology is evidence of the desire to abolish the natural ambiguity of the subject-matter – social life. In large part this inability to tolerate ambiguity in the object of study stems from the positivist leanings of sociology.

The actual practices carried on in occupational groupings called 'professions' appear disparate and related only by bureaucratic fiat and political accident. But these rather arbitrary yet bounded collections of practices provide the obvious world of practical intervention. What seems to happen at the moment is that a theory for a variety of reasons becomes fashionable and is applied as a blanket smothering the whole of the practice constel- lation indiscriminately. Thus 'phenomenological', 'behavioural' or 'conflict' approaches are advocated for controlling or demys- tifying practice in general regardless of the specific relations of the separate practices. As the prevailing mode of connection between theory and practice, or more exactly between disciplines and professions, this seems unexceptionable. But it is not inevitable, and especially if we understand paradigm change and paradigm conflict as descriptions of what generally happens rather than of what is necessarily the case in the social disciplines. It is, however, a mode which is adopted equally by the managerial apologists of conventional practices and their 'radical' critics. Particular critical approaches are taken to be total critiques of practices just as systems theory is taken to be total elucidation. For instance the versions of marxism used in *Case Con*[44] with its characteristic explanations of the role and function of the Welfare State and its prescriptions for revolutionary or pre-revolutionary action create a unity of character for state-licensed social work which may be grossly inhumane.[45] The definition, under theoretical impetus, of social work's clients as suffering only an oppressive and damaging system, and that a category of fundamental social incompetence not totally attributable to this system is a mystification of the theory, leads to prescription of only one kind of practice – collective political action. But we might say that social problems are obviously and intractably more ambiguous than this.

The increasing popularity of a systems approach is a particularly pernicious example of this theoretical closure. This is because on a commonsense basis it appears to create order out of chaos for the face-to-face social worker. It does so by means of assumptions which limit his freedom of choice of practice in two ways. First, it builds out serious differences of interest in the system being 'social worked' and thus maintains the social worker's technical authority which itself may be the problem. Second, it provides a convenient managerial rationalization for bureaucratic enlargement and domination. It is this second danger which is more likely to lead to a fixed and in the end reified series of agencies and practices which will dominate the definition of the objects of social work practice.

Structure, culture and theory

Unified and comprehensive theoretical perspectives order the relation between structure, culture and interaction by giving a priority to one level for practitioners. The most striking example of this ordering in post-classical sociology is the work of Talcott Parsons[46] in systematizing social life in a total functionalist scheme whereby all levels of action and interaction could be fitted into a seamless web, the overall character of which was in some sense a metaphysical given.[47] The aim was to make the apparently contradictory yet actually co-existing realms of social structure, cultural belief systems and day-to-day social interaction fit together by an enormous taxonomic effort. It is the degree of fit demonstrated in theory that has made Parsons's description of the social system monumentally influential. But this is a very formal success, for neither can the empirical validity of Parsons's account be demonstrated nor can the practice implications be specified beyond the maintenance of control by the possessors of the theory. It is the sociological system model *par excellence*.

But in so far as practice must take account of cultural, structural and interactional phenomena, theory for practice must be based on a plurality of accounts of alternative relations which specify alternative analyses for each sphere as well as for the relations between spheres. There has been an uneven staggering between commitments to theories holding to the structural determination of deprivation and theories directing us towards the local determination of meaning and thus control by interaction. There has been less influence from sociological theories of culture (which have taken the form largely of culture criticism) and a general shying away from open intervention in intellectual, spiritual and aesthetic affairs. This is a notable lacuna in the battery of theory available, and there is a danger that cultural matters will be seen as epiphenomenal for the interventionist professions.

The recent popularity of phenomenological theory for social workers and the less rigorous but even more influential labelling theory derived from the sociology of deviance, have raised a number of issues concerning culture which have been dropped in favour of a concentration on the interactions in which cultural meanings are played out. The treatment of culture by ethnomethodology as systems of deep rules transforms culture into an analytic notion. But for the social worker who needs criteria of evaluation as well as analysis and indeed receives them from sociology for the whole range of structural and interactional situations there is no reason why theories of cultural activity should not also provide evaluations. There is a whole area of social experience which we might refer to as culture or even as sensibility which has been addressed by schools of thought within the discipline which have not been fully incorporated into British academic sociology or which have remained arrested as a kind of descriptive cultural history.

The application of sociological theory to intervention directly or diffusely has generally produced a series of implicit directions about changing structure. In terms of deprivation and inequality, for instance, (which are meta-problems which have constituted sociology and social work) attention is directed to material resources, to the conditioning of forms of relations and to the possibilities of the control of resources and relations. But this materialist structural thrust is one which is interested and requires us to be interested in the forms of social experience rather than their content. In so far as social work can be thought of as trying to improve the content of social experience then we would expect cultural theory in sociology to become increasingly relevant.

5 Planning and social theory

Urban planning is a form of interventionist practice which has already made a subtle use of sociological theory.[1] It has been struggling since the last war for both professional status and for a disciplinary foundation which would justify an academic position. These recent circumstances provide only the most organized and dramatic examples of the repeated embrace and subsequent rejection of a variety of sociologist-provided theoretical positions. Since its inception in philanthropy, utopianism and in organized legislated civic control, planning has either been explicitly guided by theoretical convictions or its apparent pragmatism has concealed less evangelistic but none the less theoretical commitments. At the least this has taken the form of assumptions about both how individuals act socially and thus what a desirable society might look like in relation to present constraining circumstances; at the most a theoretically informed urban planning has recast its own activity from attempting to control or inspire physical development to a form of social action which is actually created by a sociological vocabulary (for instance a concern with social movements or a concern with particular kinds of population which are first made apparent or 'invented' by sociologists' theorizing activities). It is the increasing willingness of young planners over the last decade to have their professional and disciplinary vacuum filled by sociologists which makes an appraisal of the contribution of sociology particularly pertinent now. Like social workers their organizational and occupational uncertainty has made them open to conviction and conversion in an almost religious sense. The purpose of theorizing is educational and scientific, not religious, and the closure necessarily following the reification of particular theoretical approaches is the opposite of what we should hope for from sociological education.

The history of planning

There are a number of accounts of the origins and development of organized town planning[2] which treat it as a social movement with roots, in this country, in late eighteenth-century radicalism and an apex in the attempts at reconstruction and community building in the late 1940s. But the history of town planning is not an unequivocal narrative and to the extent that such a history is used we must account for the social theory which underlies it. The history of the published knowledge, the ideologies, the organizations, the individuals, the laws and the assessed consequences must be constructed. That is, the historical facts merely discipline a theory we may hold about the place of town planning in society and its relation with other institutions. Because the history of a practice is the major court of appeal to be used by apologists and activists we should be aware that the historical facts do not speak for themselves and therefore are not an obvious justification for a conviction about the social world then or now.[3] Historical conviction is really a euphemism for theoretical choice made on many other grounds than simply past events. In planning literature retrospective accounts of how planning's constricted or contradictory origins are germane to its current failure are common.[4] The more profound the criticism of planning's contemporary operation and the more a justification for failure is sought at a deep level within society, the more it requires an historical understanding. Criticisms of functioning which are pitched at the level of reform or innovation do not need to justify the intransigence of contemporary institutions at all and therefore use history only as a curiosity or as a catalogue of what has already been attempted.

There are two arguments we must be wary of in learning the 'lessons' of history. These might be called the 'inheritance' and the 'historicism' arguments. The first position tells us that all we have to work with in our own society is what we have inherited from the past[5] – that is knowledge, tools, expertise and the like which are cumulative. A variant of this argument is that position which allows for dramatically changing techniques and especially technology, but holds that these can only reflect options which have always been available and visible in the repertoire of options exercised in the past and that they can never create radically new options. These options are somehow immanently there. Thus the inheritance of the past is simply the variety of human possibilities already teased out from or attempted in an obdurate social world. We must learn the history of planning to learn the limits of what we can do and thus temper our natural propensity to utopianism. This I will call, for want of a better term, the 'liberal' lesson of history.[6] The historicism argument[7] holds that history reveals the inexorable movement of society in some direction. This process of change is fundamental and must not be confused in its depiction by the abstraction of histories of specific institutions from the wider movement. In this usage history provides the basic irreducible movement of society against which particular concerns must be projected. A history of planning in this sense has its broad limits written for it before it is researched and more particularly it has the limits of its validity pre-defined. Some kinds of marxism are obviously historicist in this way but so are many other kinds of deterministic sociological theory. Both these positions are unavoidable *to a degree*, but absolute or extreme versions of either make a virtue out of what may not be a totally constraining necessity. In other words the level at which we can see society moving in one direction and the degree to which this shift is determined are important, as is the degree to which options for intervention are somehow immanently 'there' and the extent to which our options are inherited.

The 'liberal' or meliorist history of urban planning is the story of the increasing improvement of the material living conditions of the mass of the people. It is the history of effective social reform and improvement and the gradual control of the gross physical and moral problems of industrial and urban squalor. It was incremental and humanitarian and is indexed importantly by early independent utopianism (Saltaire, New Lanark, etc.), public health and sanitation legislation, housing reform, model communities, and latterly by community planning, area renewal and social planning. This history of planning is a professional conscience which, while being well aware of the nature of a capitalist market economy, sees its job as a welfare agent guaranteeing minimum standards if not reducing differentials. There is obviously much truth in this even though it requires a commonsense view of the linkage between physical living conditions and the quality of experience. At a gross level of deprivation urban planning conceived of as a very loose social movement, which is only recently licensed by the state, can claim that it has helped many. Would anybody be prepared to argue that physical conditions in general are not better now for the mass of the population than they were a century ago, and that organized planning has not had much to do with this?[8] The case that conditions have been improved can be put while recognizing that inequalities have changed little and that planning could have done much more.

The historicist, generally marxist and determinist history of planning is the story of the incorporation of a moral social movement with diverse origins into government itself, and thus sees planning's role, in a capitalist society, as protecting private property, stabilizing markets and guaranteeing the social relations and means of production. In part this is an argument that says that the reformers and utopians claimed as ancestors by meliorists have had no significant effect on inequalities or on the nature of market society. Further, the claim is that an understanding of the nature of social change will provide the only adequate vocabulary for describing society as such, and in turn planning must be seen within this description. This view of society as at root characterized by a mode of production relegates planning to an institutional function of production. Or a view of society as a consumption system sees planning as engaged in supporting the reproduction of this consumption pattern. The irreducible core of society is the object of historical analysis and any other empirical focus will be seen in relation to it.

This situation is a warning for us. The dilemma of planning's dual origins in reform and control, and its dual interest as a moral movement and as an activity of the state, cannot be resolved by ignoring the existence of one aspect. The commentators on

83

planning when the boom in planning education and self-confidence was at its height in the early to middle 1960s[9] were optimistic at the expense of analysis of planning as a means of social control. There is a danger, now that planning is less popular and confident, that writers will throw out the baby of true amelioration with the bathwater of pessimistic historicist determinism.[10]

Planning in the system

How are we to describe the conditions under which planning as a form of interventionist practice operates? Planning is part of the state apparatus in nearly all capitalist societies. It is typical of capitalism.[11] We have recently seen the growth of a great deal of diverse commentary which because of this denies that planning can be significantly relatively autonomous and which locates planning in mixed economies firmly within the control of the three foundation institutions of capitalism – private property, profit and the market.[12] It is becoming conventional to give to planning only as much power as it is allowed by the system of which it is a part. This is a prevailing current of thought among sociologists recently. In part this is the deterministic backlash against what appeared to be the highly voluntaristic and subject-centred sociologies popular in the late 1960s and early 1970s and exemplified by phenomenological approaches.[13] The reaction has taken the form of a return to the theorizing of objects of analysis at the level of structures which many sociologists in the 1960s thought the despised characteristic of structural functionalism. The implications are wider than the sociology of planning of course. Depending upon what the system is taken to be *au fond* (production, consumption, etc.) no system part can transcend it. Education, social control, welfare delivery, leisure and so on are all seen to be engaged only in reproducing, perhaps indirectly, the dominating structural characteristic. Any other activities or effects are seen as frivolous or as unimportant anomalies.

Planning has a position within a wider and constraining 'system'. This could be described in formal constitutional terms as the organized legislature and executive. One popular version of this is to see the system as a broadly consensual and benevolent collection of decision-making and administrative bodies, not perfectly democratic by any means, but with a collection of checks and balances as democratic and responsive as it is possible to be and still get the job done.[14] We might call this the 'civil service' view of the system and it sees itself as a machine for processing problems. This is the 'charter' of the system or what the system is officially said to be for and as such is little more than propaganda. Apart from such a view the system is not describable in obvious empirical terms because like all social phenomena it is only partly visible and has to be constructed by a theory.

The two core objects which many sociologists recently take to define the system are the market and the state. The selection of such fundamental points of reference is itself a difficult area. The grounding or theorizing of particular objects and levels of objects (modes of production, modes of economic integration, etc.) is a rather circular process which is rooted either in the conviction that a particular interpretation of events is the most comprehensive or plausible available (for instance being convinced by Marx's account) or in an arbitrary manner. However they are arrived at these are predominant ways of characterizing the system in which planning operates.

Those who characterize the system as market dominated can either despise this system[15] or regard it as reasonable.[16] Either way what is being said is that the main determinants of urban development are markets in property, land and finance. The market is the major structure of allocation against which physical planning is weak. Planning cannot control or direct market forces. Planning in this context could be seen as part of the welfare state. Harvey and others[17] have looked at how the market distributes resources in a particular way and at how the welfare states have set up machinery to redistribute it by criteria of need rather than simply access to and power in the market-place. Planning is part of this welfare system which all writers have seen as merely blunting the sharpest edge of market competition. If the popular view of the welfare state is of a funnel transferring resources from higher to lower classes empirical accounts show that it is failing. Simmie's summary[18] of planning's performance in three areas crucial for potential redistribution – the location of jobs and housing; the value of property rights; the price of resources and externalities – illustrates failure. The theoretical conclusion drawn from such accounts is that welfare can only be pursued to the point at which the market is threatened, and that where 'real' welfare appears to have been delivered this has been at the cost of creating scarcity and suffering elsewhere or creating a new underclass of workers to bear the economic brunt. Planning cannot transcend the market system of which it is a part. This system is taken to be an economic one in which the social and cultural significance of the resources which are unequally and inequitably distributed are taken for granted.

The other object increasingly used to characterize the system is the state. The state is a number of institutions acting together of which the government is only one part. It broadly includes all bodies concerned with the management of social, economic and cultural activities.[19] The state is the particular focus of the continental urban marxists[20] who hold that public authorities increasingly manage the production of space and the means of collective consumption and of the more general marxist analyses of Miliband and Poulantzas.[21] At a commonsense level we are all aware of the historically accelerating extension of the state's control over major spheres of individual and communal life. At the level of economic analysis there has been a massive increase in state expenditures and investments in capitalist economies,[22] and this is only too obvious in the state's responsibility for the provision of urban infrastructure.

Within the state system planning could be seen as Pahl originally saw it as a crucial level of the management and 'gatekeeping' of resource allocation.[23] This gave to planning a high degree of power in the distribution of local resources to local authority officers and made professional planning virtually an independent variable in the urban system. In its pure form the thesis of urban managerialism implied that there was no internal logic to the state's activity beyond that implied in the professional ideology of the managers. Pahl himself swiftly crushed his own thesis[24] and was followed by others[25] in favour of the view that there was an underlying dynamic to the state's activity visible in the economic structure which it attempts to maintain, and that urban managers are at best mediators between capitalism and its victims. Their apparent power is the merest ideology. It was as if, for a moment, planning could transcend, in theory at least, the system of which it was a part. Planners' monopoly of knowledge, technical detachment and control of information gave them the crucial role of independent experts in a politically powerful position. There already existed a body of studies which had found planners' internal organization interesting for other reasons and this provided some fuel for the managerialist thesis.[26] But this was submerged by the view that the constraints of the political economy made professional activity almost redundant except as camouflage or as a form of arbitration. Planners are seen as inconsequential even where combined with other kinds of urban manager.[27]

It seems to make little difference whether the system is seen as a market or as a state. The determinism of either is great if not total and little encouragement is given to planners themselves by either view that they are or could be relatively autonomous. In the face of such pessimism the tradition of the sociology of planning which has tried to examine how planners work and what they believe seems redundant if not extravagant. Planning's own belief in its ability to create satisfactory cultural forms (community) can clearly only be the false consciousness of the life-guard who confuses waving with drowning.

Planning as a system

The urban managerialism thesis provided a rationale for the examination of planning and planners. They were believed to be a strategic group. Their replacement by other objects of analysis has left the sociology of planning with a weaker theoretical foundation. At the most we can say that their relative autonomy is problematic. But in so far as we wish to examine only those groups who have power over the deployment of capital in our society nearly all self-consciously expert or professional groups are ruled out. We do not have to believe the managerialist thesis to hold that planners are one important group among many

87

others who like most middle-level caretakers exercise some important discretionary power especially in so far as they can mobilize an ideology of professionalism and expertise. The near total determinism of those theories which reduce a complex social system to a political-economic one renders sociology itself frivolous. Yet the case studies of planning in operation seem to suggest a real and important influence at work at least at a local level.[28] This influence has generally been to oppress the poor and inarticulate, but knowing this is not enough to categorize planners as *merely* agents of higher-level more systemic oppression. Planners have been called the 'soft cops' of the system[29] but we know from studies of real policemen that the police occupy a crucial interpretive position in the social control system. At the least we need to understand the potential for planning's autonomy which could derive from its form of organization and its knowledge base.

The organization of planning reveals a series of shifts from an attempted formal professionalization into a number of alternative forms including 'deprofessionalization' and the attempted formation of a managerial and bureaucratic power base.

If we regard a profession as a group which has gained a high degree of colleague control over work processes,[30] planners become one of a number of groups which have attempted to emulate the trappings of professionalism, mistaking the control over education, credentials, codes of practice and so on for the substance of occupational self-control. The early appeal to distinct forms of technical knowledge related to but distinguishable from architecture and engineering was a prerequisite only of the status of expert.[31] It required organizational action to attempt to become a group with high status, high rewards and a monopoly over city design and development. This professionalizing activity was ironically done at the same time that planning changed from being a loosely based and reformist social movement into a fully incorporated and bureaucratic activity within the state apparatus. The perception that power for planning could only come through the organs of the state rendered the imitation of the established independent professions such as law and medicine contradictory. In no sense has planning gained for itself a professional independence which would allow it to either bargain with or within the state machinery or an independent monopoly of skill control which would allow it to dictate to other decision-makers and resource allocators. Classic professionalism is a mere cosmetic for planning.

It would be unfair to say that it is because of dashed professional hopes that the organization of planning is in disarray. The political and social convictions of many, especially young, planners is a major reason for the creation of a number of new work tasks which are still called planning. The anti-professionalism of advocacy planning[32] and community planning[33] espoused mainly by young planners and the debates within official planning about the future of the profession and of its association[34] witness the breaking up of an agreed model of organized work and the fracturing of a unified idea of what a planning 'job' is. It should be stressed that part of this schismatism is attributable to the collapse of an agreed knowledge base, but part is due to a failure of occupational self-control in a context where an employer (the state, or more precisely a local authority) was already dominating. An alternative reaction to deprofessionalization is to stress the role of sheer expertise and to claim legitimacy through technical capacity.[35] This position stresses the complexity of planning and administration in industrial society and the necessity to stay within the structures of the state.[36] In one sense this can mean a kind of bureaucratic fifth-column activity but normally it means a belief in the expert *potential* of planning. There is some backing for the belief in the possible power of the unprofessionalized or only poorly professionalized expert in government.[37] If the distributional consequences of town planning so far have suggested that little independent force has been exerted by expert planning contrary to its own ideology (and there may well be a tacit élitist acquiescence in this situation whereby planners define their activity as something else entirely than fair redistribution), this is not to suggest that planning can have no power. It may merely attest to the poor state of the art. The optimistic position which believes in some degree of autonomy must rest its case on the content of planning knowledge.

89

Historically planning has moved from a belief in the centrality of the physical environment to the view that the planned-for world was an amalgam of social, economic, political and psychological factors with no clear determinate links. From a highly focused and discrete body of knowledge planning has shifted to a very diffuse collection of relevant knowledges. This change in the knowledge base which is still at times resisted[38] involved the abandonment of a clear if crude object of analysis and field of study – architectural determinism – and the adoption of an administratively more convenient one – social policy – which was harder to pin down in academic terms. The very idea of a development plan as a form of realizable blueprint was left behind in favour of the structure plan which took the form of a loose guidance mechanism. In turn this was absorbed (before being properly adopted in practice) into 'corporate planning' and the harmonization of all local authority functions.[39] It is against this background that we can see planning's periodic bids for a knowledge base to justify its expertise.

Given that the ends of planning were expanding and blurring the major attempt for a planning-specific knowledge was pitched at a methodological level. Here through planning theory a characteristic form of procedural knowledge was adopted. A reified object had disappeared (a discrete physical environment), an alternative object was considered to be unscientific (community), so recourse was made to a reified procedure. The most famous example is the attachment to systems theory[40] which not only yielded a training technology in the form of modelling and simulation, and a quantificational grip on the world – it mystified the nature of unreconciled interests and conflicts by assuming a unified 'public' interest. The systems approach has been subject to great attack by social scientists but is resistant to real injury, and it seems likely that the lack of alternative methodologies, that is, the fact that there is no special methodology, induces a dogged refusal by planning to abandon their life raft in a situation where they have been engulfed by other better developed disciplines in all other areas. At a more abstract level we have seen attempts to give planning a character by virtue of the rationality of its methods *tout court*[41] which make it an alternative to the necessary irrationalism of the political process. This approach suggests that its very separation from politics is what gives it a distinct expertise which may involve many different techniques but which is unified at the level of grand theory. The attempt to create an expert character on the grounds of procedural distinctiveness failed for two reasons. First, that procedure itself is not discipline-specific and that for planning to declare itself a science did not mean much in a situation where all other kinds of management, intervention and policy-making said the same thing, and, second, no limitation of methods in practice (short of intuition) is dictated by such a grand level of procedural theorizing and no real professional closure was effected.

The disciplinary background and affiliation of most planners in some other discipline[42] and, increasingly, the actual content of planning education, is parasitic upon developments in other disciplines especially the social sciences.

Increasingly economics, sociology and political science provide the only distinctive theories and empirical summaries of the social situation to be planned. In a sense planning is fought over by these established disciplines, and economics, especially political economy, is winning. It is defeating a sociology concerned with cultural phenomena and the link between the material resources of peoples' lives and their felt satisfactions and sensibility. There was a short period when 'counter-cultural' planning seemed an academic possibility under the aegis of the culture criticism popular in certain kinds of radical sociology.[43] But the main thrust of the structural theorizing of Harvey, Pahl and the continental urban marxists is to treat society as a material (that is economic) system. Planning seems to be like an empty bucket which must be filled. The bucket is going to be used whatever and its emptiness does not apparently render it redundant. Thus we see an occupation's search for a discipline visible not just in the respectable and state-employed professions' hunt for an academic veneer, but also in the disaffected young planner's search for a theoretical basis to justify and articulate his inchoate criticisms of unresponsive, undemocratic and bureaucratic state inertia.

Can any of the social sciences, or some amalgam of them in the form of public administration, for instance, or regional political economy, provide enough content to nourish a planning expertise? The popularity of political economy is that it provides a critique of planning which also requires cities or urban phenomena generally to be defined away into production or into the political structures of society as a whole, especially the class struggle. It thus treats planning, defined in the state's terms, as ideological and incapable of autonomous action. It is totalizing and holistic. The older procedural theories of rational, value-free and technical resource allocation treating the planner as capable of social detachment viewed cities as objects capable of technical mastery and control by scientifically based administration, public investment and development control. If we wish to retain some form of planning function between the two extremes, some kind of expertise, albeit one parasitic upon other disciplines, we might look to sociology for a basis. Recent commentary has criticized sociology for clinging to an image which is too close to its own estimation of its authority and which mystifies and hides its real inconsequentiality.[44] Planning is seen as having its initiative progressively narrowed and is interesting only as the visible marker of underlying, obscure but powerful interests in policy. The degree to which this is true must be an empirical matter in a wider than economic sense. The failure of planning to live up to its early utopian vision and its post-war optimism may be evidence of the unrealistic and partial nature of the expectations – centring as they did around a crude and materialist notion of the 'quality of life'. The impact of planning and the area of its autonomy which we might wish to salvage from the political economic critique is that concerned with the generation of cultural expectations which have run ahead of the failure of the state to provide the material means of their satisfaction. It is the field of culture and experience which is simply assumed and untheorized by both planners and their materialist detractors alike which has been the substance of traditional urban sociology. This is in addition to the simple empirical conclusion that although planners do not systematically and collectively exercise an independent power their local effects are subject to large variations and in some circumstances they have great and fundamental influence.[45] If the variations in planning effects are as wide as Pahl admits the significance of planning, even though it be subject to more profound, even if not totally determinant, influences, remains a credible object of study. If we deny the 'pure' form of the managerialist thesis we may still be left with the 'impure' but, for interventionist purposes, significant form.

It does seem as if the urban managerialist thesis has suffered a premature demise, partly at the hands of its creator, in favour of a theoretically more profound but practically less flexible alternative.

The 'old' urban sociology

There is a body of speculations and researches which loosely constitutes 'urban sociology' for pedagogic purposes and which also has some unity as a field of study. It has until relatively recently been the source of the theoretical contribution to planning by sociologists employed as teachers, researchers or consultants. Traditional urban sociology has recently undergone convulsions which in many planners' and others' views has rendered it moribund if not dead. Its decease is attributable by its critics to its irrelevance on all scores: analytic, political and experiential. One recent critic accused most of it of embodying the irrelevant traditions of liberalism and positivism and as reflecting the varying concerns of small middle-class groups facing unprecedented city growth.[46] It is not immediately obvious that positivism and liberalism are self-evidently outmoded forms of inquiry and belief or that the historical pedigree of theories is a major criterion of their relevance.

What we might call the 'old' urban sociology is composed of a series of attempts to conceptualize what is special for sociologists in cities. It is unified only in its analytic separation of the city as an object of study. This should be emphasized because much of the objection to traditional urban sociology is that it artificially creates 'the city' and in doing so deflects the focus of research from more profound and 'real' social forces. It does not seem obvious that the mode of production is the most profound factor to be studied in social science. To accept that it is requires that we be convinced

93

on some theoretically based grounds. Even if we accept the importance of studying the institutions of the means of production this does not release us from studying the city as a historical reality and as a culturally significant phenomenon.[47] For these reasons the demise of traditional urban sociology is premature and it would be sensible to examine its use.[48]

Traditional urban sociology can be seen to fall into three strands all united by a common focus on the city as an analytically significant entity and as a phenomenon with an existential reality which is significant but not *sui generis*. That is, the city is seen in society and not simply as some isolated entity as some critics have charged.[49]

The first strand was the nineteenth-century European tradition of abstract speculation about the institutional origins and 'core' of cities as a distinct type of settlement.[50] Its form was the typologizing and classification of city types within a pre-dominantly historical framework. This was done in terms of descriptions of simple unilinear developments. Tönnies's synoptic but profound *Gemeinschaft–Gesellschaft* distinction is probably the most famous, but this was a common form for macro-sociological description to take among classical sociologists. United by an evolutionism, not always implicit, and a belief that social science was basically a form of institutional description, a variety of core institutions was presented – religion, trade, the military, etc., as the characteristic basis of the profound change of settlement types which the Middle Ages had witnessed and which the late nineteenth century was once again making dramatic. These speculations were the cradle of urban sociology. The most sophisticated example of this classical work was that of Max Weber. He proposed an ideal type description of the city as a form of settlement with a range of identifying institutional variables which were rooted in the social and economic structure of society in general. He identified changing law, administration and market conditions amongst other factors as the developmental agents of his ideal-type 'occidental' city. The city was seen as a sub-system of a changing, that is industrializing and capitalizing, society. In no sense was the city synthesized as an object of analysis. It was identified as a major marker of profound social change which once in existence exercised a profound influence for change on its own behalf. A great deal of the more recent attempts to differentiate the urban and the rural as settlement types, and especially the empirical studies of rural communities and their relationship with a wider urban society, derives from this institutional level of analysis. Contemporary community studies are not content to remain at this level of description of course and are concerned with social phenomena at the levels of interaction and group formation, differentiation and closure as well. Settlements have been shown to be internally more complex and comparatively more variegated than nineteenth-century typologies would permit. But the search for community types stems from this work.

The second strand of urban sociology and the one that has come in for most attack, both from what we can call the third strand of traditional urban sociology and from the 'new' marxist urbanology, is the social ecological school.[51] In its crude form it uses an understanding of the city as a form of struggle for space of the same kind as was understood in the early part of this century in plant ecology. The 'Chicago school' of social ecology saw the city as a sifting and sorting mechanism which obeyed natural sub-social or 'biotic' laws. The city was a gigantic selecting and distributing mechanism analogous to (and it is important to remember that it was an analogy) the organic world. Early social ecology was concerned to map out the patterns in the city, the 'natural' communities and the visible equilibria left by the competition for space. The crudeness and the sub-sociological basis of early social ecology was sloughed of in the seminal statement by Wirth[52] which can be taken to stand as the theoretical archetype of social ecological urban sociology. Wirth stated that urbanism was a distinct form of culture which comes into being when settlements increase in size, density and internal heterogeneity. The nub of the ecological case is that the city comes to have an independent existence as a social force with physical and cultural consequences attributable to it alone. The early reliance on a simplified social Darwinism and a moralizing approach to social disorganization withered away in favour of a less easily explained but more fruitfully descriptive concentration on specialization and differentiation in the city. The second strand of urban sociology cuts off the 'urban' as an analytic realm and concerns itself with the internal dynamics of the stratification and segregation of community life very largely as if the city was an independent unity. The spatial contours of a social process could be mapped but the map-makers themselves did not inquire into the deep 'geological' reasons for the features they saw. The easy excuse for the ecologists' view of a descriptive urban sociology is to say that there is obviously a level of empirical description which is not open to theoretical criticism.[53] It is simply an innocuous, theoretically insensitive but highly practical administrative activity. Plainly this would not do. The selection of differentiation, segregation or if one prefers mediated conflict rather than community formation at an institutional and interactional level requires some justification. Plainly the biological analogy has some residual force. We may disagree with this particular analogy though we cannot but describe society in analogical terms. Also what seemed to happen was that the internal dynamics of the city were deemed to be an exclusive focus and the only plausible foundation of an urban sociology. This involved a disciplinary ambition which did not hesitate to bury the earlier European foundations of urban social study.

The third strand of urban sociology is a more specifically nativist British contribution which while it formed no self-conscious school of research and scholarship at the time, can be retrospectively collected under the rubric 'urban managerialism'. The term, originally popularized by Pahl,[54] can be taken to include, primarily, that body of discussion of the gap between planning's formal ideology and its actual practice (see note 28 for examples). Basically the view held was that inequalities were generated independently of the labour market in part by the public (and private) managers of the urban system who exercised some degree of independent influence over allocation.[55] It involved positing some degree of separation between an economic system operating as an allocation mechanism and the on-the-ground functioning of bureaucracies, apparatuses and individuals who actually did the distributing. The criticism of 'pragmatic empiricism' which has been levelled at this sort of study[56] implicitly denies a theoretical focus or at least an attempt to explain the same hypotheses. This is not justified in that although not united or systematic these are a range of studies which attempt to go above the ecologists' geographical level of analysis and beneath the level of institutional, macro-sociological speculations of the European classical theories in order to examine the mechanisms of the allocation of inequality. This means that the urban is not reducible simply to the industrial but comprises a range of specific processes and relationships which are studiable and analytically separable. In terms of the accumulation of local studies this strand has had impressive results though the concentration on publicly employed managers biases its view of how power may be exercised. We can see two versions of urban managerialist theory (though it must be remembered that this 'theory' is very much a retrospective generalized account of the explanations of urban, and especially spatial, inequality rather than a specification of theoretical or research objects derived from a more abstract account of social order in general). The 'pure' managerialist thesis[57] assuming almost total control of access to local resources by local authority officers has been replaced by a more restricted version which gives them a variable degree of autonomy but which must locate this within a wider understanding of central institutions and the production and consumption of scarce resources. The second, weaker version is erected on the basis of Pahl's critique of his own work. But this critique does not eradicate the approach, as it is sometimes taken to do – it merely reduces it as a self-sufficient programme for urban sociology. The second version is a very viable basis for an urban sociology. It can be seen as the fruit of the late nineteenth-century and early twentieth-century concern with sociology as an empirical discipline which aimed to describe the conditions of citizenship under industrialism and urbanism.[58] It shares this tradition's concern with empirical analysis and with the possibility of institutional reform, and gives to sociology the task of revealing the actual as opposed to the public operation of the institutions of the state. The fact that urban managerialism has been limited mainly to planners[59] is not a necessary limitation.

The 'new' urban sociology

Over the last four or five years a small body of literature which is founded upon a dismissive criticism of all versions of the old urban sociology has become popular.[60] It is possibly a misnomer to call it a 'new' urban sociology – an anti-urban sociology would be more appropriate – in that it attempts to collapse *any* urban sociology as such, indeed any specifically urban focus, into a wider form of political economy. In effect the new version says that the old is not just a case of poor method and wrong conclusion but that its object of study – the urban – is a myth and must be abandoned in favour of more synoptic and scientific objects, such as production or consumption, within the study of which urban life (what actually happens in cities) will be made clear for the first time. On the face of things it seems unlikely that such an approach can become a rival to an established if fragmentary tradition of sociological speculation about cities. Yet increasing publications witness its muscularity.[61] How do we explain this phenomenon? Like all apparently new paradigm conflicts which are often simply examples of fashion-mongering there are both 'push' and 'pull' factors to consider.

The "pull' factors stem from a number of sources. The most important one is to do with the pedigree of this approach. The continental historical-materialist school of 'urbanology' exemplified by Manuel Castells[62] derives from the work of the marxist philosopher Louis Althusser.[63] Althusser's version of Marx's historical materialism has been taken to be one of the most cogent attacks upon and replacements for conventional sociology to emerge from marxism.[64] Since the mid 1960s in France and the late 1960s in Britain there has been an increasingly fully-fledged analytical credo and a body of practitioners concerned to replace both 'bourgeois' sociology and 'humanist' marxism. The Althusserian approach claims the status of the true science of society, a science erected on Marx's foundations and not upon an imitative and illicit empiricism. Regardless of the merits or difficulties of the Althusserian project it is in this context that Castells and subsequently numbers of other social scientists constructed an alternative analytic framework for discussing what had hitherto been taken to be urban phenomena. Thus the new approach did not have to construct a scheme of relevances and philosophical and political defences; they existed and were well articulated already. Castells and his colleagues were simply applying the ideas of what had by the early 1970s already become a social and political as well as a scholarly movement. It is important however to realize the attraction of the Althusserian claim to be *the* science of society and to be marxism.[65] The evangelical claim of science for the social disciplines has been apparently irresistible since Comte. Little wonder then that a claim in an area which has already dallied with ecological 'science' should exert such an attraction. Marxism in various forms has, especially since the 1960s, been seen by many sociologists as less a resource than an alternative form of social study. The iconic status of Marx's texts and the theology resultant upon their interpretation have provided a respectable basis for a number of alternative accounts of social fundamentals. The pedigree of Althusserianism and thus of Castells is impressive.

The popularity of the materialist approach to urbanism only became so in Britain with the translation of some of Castells's simpler texts in the mid 1970s. The publication of his major work,[66] which is much more complex, dense and confused, has ironically only been undertaken in Britain when his approach was already quite popular. Although there are numbers of other continental materialists who share Castells's views to a variable extent, there is little British research interest inspired by this approach as yet, though there is a great deal of theoretical and speculative work.

The 'push' factors explaining why such an approach should be popular now mostly relate to the over-reaction to social ecology and the premature closure of urban managerialism. A vacuum has been created which a historical-materialist approach appears to fill. Although Castells himself took the social ecology of Louis Wirth and its aftermath as the exemplary target for his marxist criticism, he has been used in this country to criticize urban managerialism and what has been called the Weberian position,[67] which stresses the role of bureaucracy in the distribution of life

99

chances. A disenchantment with the additive approach of managerialist case studies and the impact of Gouldner's attack on the sociological exposés of 'middle dogs' and 'caretakers' rather than 'top dogs',[68] which mystifyingly seemed to carry a great deal of moral weight in the early 1970s, had the combined effect of creating a body of sociologists who were critical of the prevailing and available theoretical positions but with nothing to offer in their place. Deeper than this perhaps is the reaction to the British empiricist tradition in general which British sociologists began to experience in the late 1960s. This is instanced in one sociologist's summary of the sins of traditional British urban sociology by 'élitism', 'technocratism', 'liberal pragmatism', 'social democratism' and 'positivism'.[69] The same author says that it is agreed that traditional urban sociology is valueless.[70] There is no doubt that there was in the early 1970s a prevailing dissatisfaction with urban sociology as comparatively poorly developed in its theory and muddled in its application. It was, as it were, ripe for a takeover by a new approach which would totally redefine it. To some extent we must look at the organization of sociologists to explain changes in academic fashion. We must also look at the merit of the ideas themselves.

Put simply the new approach is founded on the belief that to accord any autonomy to the realm of the urban in social science is to elevate an administratively derived unit to the status of a fundamental social reality. 'Urbanism' and 'urbanization', which are basic terms in traditional urban sociology, are not things in themselves and neither do they have explanatory adequacy. They are ideological terms and the urban sociology which depends upon them and takes as its task the elucidation and explanation of them has no scientific status. In the jargon of this school urban sociology as practised by ecologists or institutional theorists has no 'urban theoretical object' which would justify its scientific pretensions. (This same criticism, of course, would apply to many other specialist sociologies.) Thus until now urban sociology has been a series of administrative aids providing useful information for urban governance but having no justifiable social scientific theory. The various theories which have existed (Weber, social ecology, urban managerialism) have been attempts to gloss this situation and inject a theoretical justification. For Castells and those who follow him science is historical materialism by definition. The fundamentals of social life, they believe, are material and it is the contradictions revealed within the material structure of capitalism and the secondary cultural and political contradictions that provide the social life which we must analyse. The Althusserian problematic which is the basis of this view provides a vocabulary and a highly complex analytical scheme within which society can be theorized at an abstract and structural level.

For Castells neither space nor built form itself are independent or even partially autonomous factors. Crudely, the city does not have effects − it does not cause anything. What is meant by the city is a particular form of organization of collective consumption. What we are really studying is the structure of capitalism, the class struggle and the role of the state, all of which are articulated through and within cities. Thus empirical analyses[71] focus on the institutions of monopoly capitalism (for instance the conflict between the different kinds of capital), the analysis of oppositional urban social movements and the description of the state's enabling activities in developing particular areas. Overall this approach, as Mellor notes,[72] holds that community life and buildings cannot be abstracted from the productive and political relations of capitalism. In this many members of the new school see themselves as returning to classic nineteenth-century concerns of the relation between cities and developing capitalism. Although Pickvance suggests that historical materialist approaches are supplementary to general urban sociology,[73] and although Harloe suggests we can accept Castells's formulations without accepting the work of Althusser on which they are based,[74] it is hard to see the new approach to urban life as anything other than a replacement form of study which can in no way accept or use any of traditional urban sociology.

Before turning to an assessment of the new approach we might note its increasing diversification. Within its broad conversion of urban sociology to political economy there is arising a rather watered-down version in which the full panoply of historical materialism is ignored. Rather the materialist basis of society is used as a context within which the activities of, for instance, bureaucracies, experts and the effects of local peculiarities can be examined. Pahl and Mellor are examples of this.[75]

This seems to be a schism which denies the exclusive claims of the Castellsian position to truth and scientificity. The very claims to truth of historical materialism disallow the importing of a Weberian or any other problematic. Such mixing of theoretical positions is not allowed. Yet Pahl and Mellor use the insights of the marxists into the economic formation and more importantly use the technical vocabulary of marxism, stressing basic processes such as reproduction of the relations of production and the role of the state. But they then insert this technical language into a revived concern with managerialism (Pahl) and regional development (Mellor) and in general use it to highlight the very *bête noire* of the materialist, localism. There is a variety of the new urban sociology stretching from the out-and-out structuralist marxism of Castells to the residual managerialism and localism of Pahl and Mellor.

A full-scale criticism of the Castellsian position could only be erected on a full-scale criticism of its Althusserian assumptions.[76] The avid theoreticism and structural abstraction pose great problems for empirical research. One vitriolic reviewer who was herself almost alone in rejecting traditional urban sociology's parochialism twenty years ago[77] has called Castells's work 'absurd' and 'a load of humbug',[78] and certainly its denseness and neologistic style provide the ideal environment for the breeding of mystification and ambiguity. But the basic criticism we could apply to this work is that it is unable to dispense with the very concept which it is pledged to bury – that of the urban. Its status is redefined by Castells by fiat but its manifest reality as a social object as well, therefore, as an object of analysis continually reasserts itself in his and his colleagues' work. It thus appears as a form of logical system building, a wholly theoretical discourse into which reality which can be researched cannot be recognized. Indeed, in so far as empiricism itself as a form of research is abandoned by this school, research becomes only a matter of theoretical elaboration. At the level of epistemology then the Castells extreme of the new urban sociology presents grave problems.

In terms of the key concept by which what goes on in cities is made comprehensible in the context of political economy, namely 'collective consumption', there are also difficulties. Pahl has examined the possible meanings of collective consumption in the continental urban materialists' work and comes to the conclusion that collective consumption has no reference to any specific mode of production such as capitalism and is close to becoming a functionalist banality.[79] In so far as the city is seen as a unit of collective consumption and the state is seen to dominate in its organization and control we find ourselves simply talking about the structure and control of cities as we always have done within traditional urban sociology. In so far as state intervention is variable in advanced industrial societies we merely have an argument for detailed and comparative studies of urban management. The real nub is whether we are content to view that management as totally determined by the inexorable logic of the development of capitalism. In other words we are back to questions about the autonomy of the urban and of the managers of the urban realm. The Castellsian position dictates a form of complex but none the less economic determinism which renders all questions of empirical variation only of peripheral interest. The basis of understanding cities is dictated by the acceptance of the theory of historical materialism alone.

Planners and sociological theory

Sociological theory for planners has been very important. The old and the new urban sociologies have been the vehicles of theories basic to planners' conception of their object of practice and their avowed discipline. Yet too often theorizing has had the effect of restricting and narrowing practice. The gradual decay of the conception of the planned-for world as a purely physical environment, however, is a sign of the power of theorizing. Theorists have not inspired this change but their work has helped and guided planning towards a more varied conception of policy and action. The 'new' urban sociology however is no less exclusive and limiting in its theoretical prescriptions for practice than the old. Unlike the old it explicitly relegates all ideas of the autonomy of urban culture. The concern with culture which was the very point of critics' dissatisfaction with the community studies tradition can be seen to be one of the major characteristics of a sociological approach. To the extent that the new urban sociology denies this culture, to that extent a political economy replaces sociology. A pluralism of theory is necessary for a continued concern with culture and interaction as well as structure and institution.

6   Social theory for intervention

Sociology is an interventionist discipline. It is interventionist in that from its institutional beginnings it has been concerned with practical affairs in society. It is a discipline in that from its ideological beginnings it has adopted a formal framework for the acceptance and rejection of knowledge. It is built on this paradox which is reflected in its most acute form in the apparently irreconcilable demands of theory and practice. In this chapter I want to describe some of the complexities of a discipline which serves these two masters, complexities which now threaten to destroy sociology as a coherent form of knowledge with a distinctive type of content and with an object of study which is significant in society's own terms.

The discipline of sociology

Sociology is more than social thought. As a discipline, it has an institutional existence, primarily within education and research organizations, which attempts to control standards of acceptability and the forms of that thought. It is a community[1] or, if one prefers, a number of communities. It is anchored in social organization. The community is not isolated, however, and the discipline is directed outward to an audience, as well as developing an internal dialogue. This audience is not a collection of passive spectators but comprises a number of separate audiences who *use* sociology and ask it questions. They range from policy-makers concerned with the solution of the technical administrative problems of the state, through particular groups who actually suffer these problems, to the individual who demands above all else an enlightenment of his experience.

Historically, sociology has always addressed such users, especially in the Anglo-Saxon tradition of sociology.[2] Even the most apparently academicist of sociologies addresses such 'clients'[3] and the most scholarly dialogues are preludes to dialogues between scholars and other users. In this respect, then, sociology is not and has not been a 'pure' discipline and it is not a formal discipline in the sense that mathematics or logic are. Of course, it has aspects which require formalism and styles which assume purity but they are not themselves constitutive or regulative of the form of knowledge of sociology.

The notion that sociology is a 'practical' discipline is widely held even between divergent schools. But the precise nature of its connection with social interests is a real bone of contention. At their most sophisticated, debates about the action implications of sociology take the form of denunciations of such a contamination. From Hegelian Marxism critics attempt to purify the discipline of its implicit technocratism by addressing an abstract humanism.[4] From historical materialism, writers try to define an immanent global and universal social interest which transcends the mundane.[5] At its crudest, specific administrative problems are promoted as master interests to which the discipline must be tailored.[6] There are a variety of conceptions of users and levels of interests.

There are also a variety of forms which the discipline takes. In fact, so great is this variety that their combination into a 'discipline' might seem impossibly optimistic. Indeed, were we to take seriously the idea that a discipline is unified solely by its common 'object',[7] whether 'real' or 'technical', we should give up the game and begin afresh. But, given that such objects are not natural categories (apprehendable, that is, without a theory) and given that academic practices have institutional bases, traditions and, generally, communities of practice in common, we would do well to disallow common objects as the fundamental arbitrators of disciplines. Within such a sociological community a number of competing, colliding and co-operating approaches can be seen. Historically, and in the present, the fact of pluralism within sociology is undeniable, but the forms of accommodation of such a pluralism are open to debate. Recently we have seen notable attempts to destroy particular variants, especially functionalism at the level of theory, empiricism at the level of methodology and liberalism-meliorism at the level of political intervention. Does a discipline require a monism by definition or can it permit and exploit a pluralism?

It is out of the variety of interests and forms that the central problems of the discipline have emerged. Very broadly, these are three: problems about the status of social phenomena as real phenomena – problems of ontology; problems about the status of the knowledge we produce about social phenomena – problems of epistemology; problems about why we are producing this knowledge or how it is to be used – problems of the relation between theory and practice.[8]

What we see now in sociology is a battle between schools of thought wishing to elevate one kind of problem to pre-eminence. More particularly, one can read the history of sociology over the last two decades as the attempt to subdue the third problem area – the relation between theory and practice – and this is especially true within that area of sociology which we might call 'sociological theory'.[9]

Increasingly, debates within sociology are exclusively philosophical and formalist and there seems little guarantee that they will in the end help our action. There is, of course, no indication that they hinder our action either and I do not wish to condemn philosophy. But I do wish to condemn the hypocrisy of many of those sociologists who plead service to mankind by theoretical criticism without relating theory to practices in a real world.

Theory and practice in general

It is plain that a concept of 'pure' knowledge is impossible.[10] Knowledge is an instrument constituted by human and social interests. The demonstration by Rescher[11] that all purely rational justification of our standards of factual truth are illusory is persuasive for sociology to the extent that sociologists believe their knowledge to be factual. Fay shows that, with regard to positivism and interpretive social science, what will count as knowledge is justified by at least an implicit relating of theory to practice.[12] Habermas believes that these interests resolve to only three – technical control, mutual understanding and the emancipation from the natural.[13] Our theorizing is trapped by our practice. Denial of this, as is the case in 'pure' physical science, is an illusory self-understanding which justifies freedom from accountability.

Yet all disciplinary knowledge is also theoretical in that it involves abstraction and generalization.[14] Theory is inevitable. It may remain implicit or inarticulate, it may be arrested at the level of justifying dogmas or unexplained values, but theory is as rooted in the notion of 'thought' as practice is in the concept of 'society'. There are broadly three positions adopted with respect to the general relation between theory and practice in sociology. (This requires that we ignore for the moment that position which is explicitly anti-theoretical, for instance, some crude forms of pragmatism, purely statistical empiricism, 'grounded theory', etc.) The first position is that which distrusts theory and, in a mild sense, is anti-intellectual. Here only action is really valid and it is better to act badly than not to act at all. Theory is often used in this style as a rhetorical gloss and is arrested at an almost purely descriptive level. An example might be the role of behaviouralism in the 'policy' social sciences generally. Theory is used as a cosmetic which gilds the underlying incrementalism, rationalism and managerialism which, no doubt, could be theoretically explicated and justified but which instead are often masked.

The second general position is that which proclaims the mutual penetration of theory and practice, either in the form of *praxis*[15] and so-called 'critical theory' or in the form of 'theoretical practice'.[16] A variety of specific discussions attempt to destroy by definition the distinction between theory and practice in a utopian way. There are great acrobatics involved in this area which we will deal with later.

A view of theory and practice which dictates the priority of theory is possible. Without abrogating some superior directing power to theorists, similar to that which Mannheim gave to his 'free-floating intelligentsia', we can adopt the position that theory is the necessary precursor of action, that failure to theorize before acting leads to incoherent and inconsistent action, and that a great deal of work needs doing in laying down the parameters of theoretical discussion which will enable specific forms of practice to 'work'.[17] There are a number of examples of theorists who are concerned with specific forms of practice and who theorize accordingly.[18] I hold the view that theory is powerful, that it can proscribe, prescribe and permit action within specifiable limits, and that a history of particular forms of practical activity (such as planning) will reinforce this view.

There are interesting and ignored lessons in the history of British and American sociology. The reading of the history of sociology as the history of its theory, especially of its epistemological concerns, is not the whole story. In Britain, academic sociology grew in part from an early concern with meliorism and efficient charity, which were devoid of theoretical unity, towards a coalescence of scientific ideas and social action.[19] There is unjustified neglect of the British tradition of liberal social science which seems connected with the popular belief in the failure of reform *per se*.[20] In the USA, where the tradition of philosophical pragmatism is stronger,[21] there is less of a pressure towards metaphysics. The compromise reached between institutional demands and the internal development of theoretical concerns has had more authority there. A notable example is the development of the 'Chicago School'.[22] However, we should not be blind to the sell-out as well as to the compromise, and the development of 'policy science' illustrates the more absurd reaches of a social science which abandons theory for governmental interest.[23]

Recent developments

The most important developments within sociology have recently seemed to come from debates about theory and meta-theory. They are important in two senses; they have had the greatest impact on sociology's only captive clients – its students – and they have questioned the previously often assumed simple relationship between the discipline and policy-making. The most publicized versions of new 'critical', 'materialist' and 'phenomenological' sociologies seem, on reflection, to fail to solve disagreements about relativism and the nature of social intervention. They offer no real advance, but they are popular for the way their new vocabularies fill the space left empty by the absence of a theory concerned with practice. Such new alternatives are sometimes misleadingly aggregated as 'critical'.[24]

They are alternatives to each other as well as to the targets they seek to replace,[25] but they should not be dismissed outright as irrelevant by opponents. They have posed the most important questions about social intervention in a clear and valuable way.

Phenomenological sociology has defined for us the danger of assumptions about the transcendental nature of consciousness.[26] It has illustrated most clearly the point at which a theory will dictate non-intervention as the price to be paid for asking questions which we know in advance are incapable of decisive answer. Its attraction may be that it treats all men as theorists; its cost is that no phenomenologist may attempt to define a social problem. Let us be clear. Phenomenology does not mystify the relation between theory and practice as some other sociologies do, it merely bids practice wait for the solution of ontological and epistemological problems. Many sociologists who recognize the problems of 'rationality' in description remain unconvinced by the promise of the 'constitutive phenomenology of the natural attitude'[27] clarifying 'modes of being-in-the-world',[28] especially as we find ourselves in a world where others will definitely act even should we choose to remain passive. Not surprisingly, phenomenological sociology has had the least real impact on interventionist sociology of any of the recent developments.

The rise in interest in 'critical' sociology is more closely tied to the theory/practice link. Based upon the unexceptionable view that particular forms of theory (e.g. positivism) and particular forms of interest (e.g. technical domination or control) are inevitably enmeshed, it has attempted to create a category of theory − dialectical and hermeneutic − which will permit a pure *praxis* unalloyed with any technical cognitive interest.[29] Central in this field is the diverse work of the 'Frankfurt School'[30] which stretches, in the immediate and popular form, from the mystical anti-science of Marcuse[31] to the anti-logical Habermas.[32] The major impact of 'critical' sociology has been to mystify and fetishize the theory–practice relation. The Hegelian Marxism of critical theorists has sought to develop a socialist self-consciousness[33] freed from 'restricted rationality'.[34] This will be done, in one version, 'dialectically', that is by uniting theory and practice and transcending the dualism of cognition and evaluation.[35] Sociology of this critical kind seeks a realm of experience, questions about which cannot be answered by 'technically utilizable information' and 'are not capable of explanation by empirical, analytical enquiries'.[36] 'Hermeneutics', which is the methodology chosen, adopts an alternative transcendental notion of the social on a basis which offers no acceptably greater degree of ontological certainty.[37] In short, 'critical theory', 'dialectics' and 'hermeneutics' are used by the Frankfurt sociologists to transform the practical into one specific form of practice, namely, the changing of consciousness into a critical tool by which the material world will itself, in turn, be changed. This is a replacement for a social science which would abandon intervention short of the one activity prescribed by the theory. 'Theoretical disputes with "bourgeois science" can be maintained *in practice* only as a form of the class struggle',[38] and the academic is elevated to that practice *par excellence*.

The popularity of the historical materialist attempt to create a materialist 'science' to replace the 'ideologies' of the existing social disciplines is another recent major development in (or attack on) sociology. Based on the difficult work of Althusser[39] it exemplifies the 'primacy of practice' principle. It seeks to elaborate the philosophical basis of historical materialism in order to reconstitute those disciplines which misperceive their 'real' grounding in our society. This has practical implications.[40] Its attractions are that it explains the failure of past disciplines and recreates their real practices in terms of new interventions. This seems plausible in that it claims new apprehensions of the 'objects' of a discipline. Thus, existing sociology is seen to fail because it is only a pseudo-discipline and has objects of study which are unreal or myths. It also fails because its empiricism allows it knowledge (which, Althusser says, exists in the realm of thought) to be validated only by a comparison with 'facts' (in the realm of the real). That is, empiricism of any kind relies on the illicit comparison of phenomena in two different logical orders. The test of knowledge lies only within the process of the production of that knowledge.[41] The search for a unifying and meta-theoretical standard lies not within positivism, humanism, historicism or even within epistemology itself.[42] It lies within a conception of practice conceived as a process of production by labour. The conceptions of knowledge and science that historical materialism holds are constituted at root by a reliance on a particular reading of Marx which is deemed by its reader, Althusser, as unverifiable. There are profound difficulties in grounding or authorizing the Althusserian project which are beyond the scope of this book.[43] But the immediate impact of this approach is to question the objects of analysis. Thus, for instance, within urban sociology urbanism itself is rejected as a myth and is replaced by two more realistic objects – the production of space and the processes of collective consumption.[44] What is puzzling is the criterion for selecting these two new foci for the discipline. Why are they more appropriate than the administrative object they replace? What is the reason in theory and in practice for elevating the state as the prime focus? The selection of this object rather than some other slab of reality rests upon the demand by historical materialism that its own criteria are superior, even though a demonstration of this superiority is treated as irrelevant and ideological within the approach itself.

Historical materialism is a totalizing approach. It asserts that everything is related to everything else, that this is more complex than either humanist or vulgar determinist marxisms would have us believe, but that there are principles of operation of the structures which make up this complex totality. This is understandably an attraction. Sociologists have long realized that the *analytic* segregation of social structures and processes is a problem. But, in terms of practice, it is a trivializing truth for it makes all interventions but 'total' ones irrelevant and, thus, treats all social problems which cannot be explicitly related to class struggle as superficial.

Having said this, and making plain that as an exclusive claim to science historical materialism is incomprehensible, the heuristic use of the 'primacy of practice' framework and the conceptions of real and unreal objects of analysis are useful analytically.[45]

My point is that all three recent fashionable developments in sociology treat social intervention and the attempt to define and ameliorate social problems as trivial. They depart radically from the tradition of sociology as an interventionist discipline.

The commitments of sociology

If we assume that we do not want to collapse sociology into philosophy and that we believe that there is some mileage in it, what must its commitments be? The search for a pre-suppositionless sociology can have no commitment to intervention. If we want intervention, we must commit ourselves to a practical object before we begin to theorize about it. This does not say very much. Merely that the *raison d'être* of sociology is practice and that theorizing, analysis and other action are secondary to this.

But we know that below this level any specific notions of practice, specific locations and immediacies, etc., taken as the reason for sociology, are the result of the theories held.[46] The circularity of theory and problem definition cannot be escaped except by fiat.[47] In a significant sense the existence of sociology relies upon the assumption of a variety of absolutes which are untheorized, otherwise we would simply be involved in a formless relativism or a search for a natural order. Choosing the object of analysis (goal, problem, issue, practice, etc.) is inevitable. The operative criteria are moral and political. Plainly to derive a theory of the good and the efficient from a study of what exists can no longer be seen to be the primary task of the social disciplines, unless we abandon the idea of intervention and play a waiting game in which theoretical certainty must arrive before practice can begin.

The primacy of suffering

If we can agree that sociology must presume, as it originally did, a concern with practice and intervention, what substantive focus

113

should it adopt? Put differently, if we agree that philosophical and academic concerns are not acceptable as primary standards for judging theories, what are acceptable?

All that is proposed here is a rationale for a particular direction in which sociology could develop.

Sociology is classically founded on a concern with happiness and suffering. In the British tradition of social philosophy, the utilitarians occupy a central position. Recently such standards have been given eloquent backing by Barrington Moore.[48] His concern is to direct social inquiry towards an understanding of the institutional causes of gross human suffering – war, cruelty, hunger, want, injustice and oppression. He leap-frogs over the self-serving problem-definitions of liberalism and marxism in order to show that such misery is widely occurring across societies and varied social organization. In the face of the unitary nature of human suffering, he says, the primary concern over the proper role of moral evaluation in a discipline is unjustified.[49] There are broad constants in the problem of human misery which were the concern of classical European sociology and which were also the concern, less articulately, of much neglected consideration in Britain before the academic sociology 'explosion'.

The disaggregation of the concept of human misery is a very plausible substantive basis for sociological theory. It would also, as Tudor has recently pointed out,[50] be a basis for rescuing the insight of much theoretical work which would otherwise become mere fodder for the schisms and fragmentations which characterize the academic sociology world. For instance, the specification of human suffering as problems in the two broad areas of *survival* and *sensibility* would be macro-concerns which straddle all social and political arrangements, and seem, anyway, to be the exhaustive categories into which practical sociological interests have naturally fallen.

The place of theory

The abandonment of a search for a meta-theory in favour of a meta-problem still leaves us with the problem of specifying the kinds of theory appropriate for classifying types of social practice as concrete sites of analysis and intervention. This, one might suggest, is less a matter of erecting a new theory as an alternative 'school' of the discipline, than salvaging what is relevant in the theoretical work we already have. There are enough 'new' sociologies around with grandiose claims. What it may be possible to do is to lay out the manner in which existing sociologies self-consciously classify practice and, thus, judge their potential for intervention.

This means using theories as a resource for intervention when the actual locations of intervention are not decided beforehand by administrative fiat or by political concern. I am not suggesting that theoretical work is to be seen as a tool of policy or protest. It is to be seen as a mechanism allowing policy and protest to be linked by elaborating the connections between the conceptual schemes existing within the various theories. At the moment, theory is a battleground. Each theory claims to locate problems afresh, and to possess an overriding truth. The constructive potential of sociology is spent in internal criticism, recrimination and destruction. A pluralism of theory, baldly proposed, seems a weak and vapid alternative unless there is some principle uniting the apparent divergences. That principle could be the specification of intervention to relieve suffering.

As a first step, it is necessary to catalogue the raw material we have to work with: our theories. A list of theories (or 'approach paradigms' as Bernstein would prefer to call them)[51] would yield a crude inventory of 'objects' of analysis, or more precisely limits to the level of object admitted as relevant. This could be illustrated in tabular form. What is striking is the 'object-boundness' of distinct theoretical approaches (see Table 1).

Any conviction that levels of objects of analysis are connected cannot rest content with the blanket application of one approach. The selection of approaches must be ordered by some view of the connectivity of the levels. It is not enough to say that all is 'built up' from consciousness or that all is 'predicted down' from total structure as justifications for remaining at any one level.[52]

The second step after cataloguing the approaches is to specify principles of connection. Increasingly, single theories themselves

Table 1

Examples of 'theories' or 'approach paradigms'	Level of object of analysis
Evolutionism 'Scientific' marxism Structuralism	Total system
Structural functionalism Systems theory	Social structure
Frankfurt 'critical' theory Weberian idealism Structuralism	Culture
Exchange theory Role theory Behaviourism	Behaviour
Phenomenological sociology 'Critical' theory	Consciousness

have been seen to provide these principles, usually by giving an account of absolute meanings or ultimates as maps of the total terrain.[53] But these are only moral and metaphysical maps. The belief in a principled pluralism in sociology means that we commit ourselves not to a theory in the theological or doctrinal sense we have been used to but to the meta-problem as a means of connecting widely different approaches. Theoretical

Table 2   Problems of suffering

Level		Survival	Sensibility
Societal	Problem	Astro-physical and biological survival	Pluralism and heterogeneity
	Theory	Evolutionism	Functionalism
Group	Problem	Justice and efficiency	Communality
	Theory	Exchange theory	Interpretative or 'critical' theory
Personal	Problem	Freedom from want	Sense of competence
	Theory	Psychological theory	Symbolic interactionism

'triangulation'[54] is made possible by a concern with a meta-problem. Theories are not ends in themselves but are a means of achieving a grip on practice. Therefore they can be used, not eclectically, but in a principled methodological fashion. See Table 2.

Thus, the boundaries of any particular empirical issue of suffering are not fixed. This means paying more than the usual lip service to the rest of the world while attention is actually limited to smaller and smaller issues at one particular level. It means locating the issue within a range of levels as an initial analytic task. In this way we make use of theory in sociology in so far as it has addressed substantive as well as purely formal issues.

The utopianist collapse of theory and practice into one ideal praxis, the impotence of pure theory, and the unreflective pragmatism of a theoryless social study must all be avoided. To pursue intervention, a time-ordering of theory and practice must be adopted. Intervention is the subject of the exercise and, thus, theory must serve this end. Theoretical work which halts or bars action may be interventionist in the wider sense used here as long as it is substantive theory. That is, for instance, it may require only more analysis or more classificatory work as its practice. It does not, however, rule intervention out of court because it refuses it as a relevant disciplinary category.

The false dichotomies of, for instance, 'sociologies of opposition' and 'sociologies of decision'[55] are harmful in that they reduce the criteria of a discipline into its commitment to a particular constructed object − the state − which is no more a 'natural' category than any other. Also, sociology devoted to criticism rather than to construction is the result, with the consequent popular devaluation of sociological insight which has become so familiar. Sociology is one of the major vehicles of social criticism our sort of society possesses.[56] But when this critical function is transformed into an exclusive critique which replaces what it rejects with nothing but vague utopias it becomes false to society.

It is probably the case that 'sociologies of ...' or 'sociologies in ...' courses, as presently taught within sociological education, often uncritically reflect existing administrative arrangements

117

(e.g. the sociologies of industry, education and law). There has been, in reaction to this, a shift rejecting all such disciplinary segmentation as reification, and attempting to focus on 'deeper' levels of social reality which dissolve the divisions of the everyday administrative world. The recent changes in the definition and intentions of urban sociology are a good example;[57] others might be the 'new' sociologies of education and deviance. In most cases these moves have not only been away from a subservient position for sociology but also a movement towards a stance which permits little decisive intervention in the short or medium term. The revelation and demystification seen as the dynamics of such changes exercise their own domination as a substitute for any attempt at reform. That many of the objects of sociological analysis were untheorized in any way is true. But the shift away from this position has gone too far with the result that analysis itself is now very often its own client.

Sociology can be applied to contexts outside of itself and an attempt made to classify these contexts. The principles of coherence and consistency in such a classification are logical in the first place, of course, and then empirical in response to a theory of practice.

Theoretical classification only gives us the potential for intervention which is built into the status of the theory's object. Theory cannot, in reality, create the world: it can only help in explaining what we have chosen to be interested in. Intervention must begin at some point and the most plausible starting-points are the formal institutions (of production, control, administration, etc.), the sectional interests (in life chances, distribution, etc.), and in the generalized audiences (for enlightenment and the intrinsic importance of analytic understanding). If sociology is not to become split between romantic utopianism and total quietism reformism is the only strategy left. Theory appropriate for reformist practice will have to be more modest and more committed than hitherto.

Theoretical pluralism

Much of what has been said begs an important question, namely, what is the advantage of the co-existence of a number of theoretical approaches in sociology – or why pluralism? I have explicitly advocated a principled pluralism of theory and the desirability of maintaining (though refining) the inventory character of sociological theory which so many sociologists find exasperating. But I have only implicitly justified theoretical pluralism as such.

There are two senses in which we can talk about theoretical pluralism. There is the very precise, technical sense described by Klima[58] as 'real' pluralism where a number of rival theories (fully connected with observables and fully logically elaborated, that is using 'theory' in the very strict sense) contradict each other and where only one of these theories can be true. Sociological theories are generally insufficiently rigorously formalized to permit us to recognize any cases of 'real' pluralism in sociological theory, and in any case this kind of pluralism is really only a stage on the way to a theoretical monism. The canons of empirical science will not permit a number of theories with logically contradictory postulates to predict the same outcome. We can, presumably, dispense with this sense of the term for sociological theory as we know it.

One variant of this position is the strategic pluralism suggested by a number of philosophers of science, notably Feyerabend,[59] (and in a less anarchistic form by Lakatos).[60] This is an advocacy of the bombarding of problems by as many theories as possible in the belief that competition will only stimulate. Again pluralism is merely used as an efficient and purposeful method of elimination, a staging post on the way to theoretical truth (or closure).

The second sense is that used by Merton[61] in attempting to account for and protect diversity and the clash of doctrines generally within sociology. This refers to what is often seen as paradigm conflict in sociology; not just the contradiction of theories predicting the same outcome but the presentation of a variety of *problems* and *phenomena* for investigation – if one prefers the diversity of problematics themselves. There is no implicit 'market' or 'competition' structure for theory (as Klima, Feyerabend and Lakatos would like to see) but a variety of incommensurable markets. This is pluralism as an end rather than as a means.

It is important not to get these two senses confused. The impact of discussions in the philosophy of science which have crystallized as arguments about the paradigmatic status of sociology as a discipline have accepted versions of the first sense of pluralism discussed here. This sense is certainly embedded in Kuhn's work and has resulted in what Merton calls the 'Doctrine of the Single Paradigm'.[62] The acceptance, not only of the conclusion, but of the usefulness of the whole debate must rest on the degree of formalization of sociological theory – actual and possible. In the absence of such formalization, and plainly it is absent, the debate must become more than purely methodological. It is, of course, possible to read Kuhn's concept of 'paradigm' as embodying the second sense of pluralism mentioned above but the development of a discussion about the propriety of such pluralism (i.e. of paradigms) would depend upon different criteria compared with a debate concerned only with 'real' or 'strategic' pluralism. In other words we must decide whether pluralism is an end in itself in sociology or is a means to a monism.

The major argument for pluralism as the desirable state of the discipline is a moral one. If it is a disease the cure would be much worse. Total theoretical closure, a directed monism, would be appalling in a discipline which we realize has more than a cognitive character. Socially and politically there is no case to be made for an interventionist discipline disavowing pluralism unless recourse is made to a Comtean positivist version of the planned society in a totally determined universe. Even a minimal and fragmentary belief in the analytic importance of voluntarism and emergence destroys the attraction of the anti-pluralist position.

In discussions about the desirability of theoretical pluralism it is often unclear to me whether a pro-monist line is being taken because of the conviction of the ultimate truth of one particular theoretical approach, or because of a distrust of pluralism as such. The distrust is usually on the grounds that it dissipates energy and therefore retards progress, or that pluralism is merely an ideology which camouflages tyranny by an inappropriate theory, usually to the benefit of the powerful. I have already introduced my

120

objections to the first position. The second stance (pluralism as ideology) is substantial and deserves a fuller treatment than is possible here. The basic position is that pluralism is said emphatically not to exist in that while proliferation of theories as such is permitted and often encouraged only particular kinds of *theory-in-practice* are allowed. The state, for instance, is said to use academic pluralism to mask its underlying manipulative theoretical concerns, and public policy and social control are founded upon only particular dominant theoretical perspectives.

A reply to this argument might be that even if this was and is the case that is still not a criticism of pluralism itself. It is an implied request for a more thorough-going and self-conscious theoretical pluralism which can at least complicate state-funded theoretical positions within institutions of higher education and research. Or it is a call for an alternative theoretical monism, appropriate to different interests perhaps, but which requires a closure of theory none the less. It is a call for abandoning the 'pretence' of pluralism, and if this is unacceptable the problem simply reasserts itself.

No defence of pluralism can proceed without an analysis of the distribution and exercise of power, of the character of reform as a type of social change and the meshing of theory with prescriptions for social change. I hope to look at some of these issues more fully elsewhere.

The importance of pluralism

It is probably true that all disciplines or 'subjects' or bodies of knowledge are pluralisms which are in various states of tension. At the most dramatic dissent is never completely prevented and at the most innocuous we can only communicate over a significant period of time by agreeing to disagree about many important things. So plainly what we need to consider is the variety of modes of pluralism in sociology.

I have just accounted for why I think pluralism should be encouraged, not the least because this would make a virtue of a necessity. This inevitable character of sociology is a resource which should be traded upon. A sociology of knowledge approach to sociological knowledge has been shown to illuminate our understanding of the range of sociological traditions and styles[63] and their conditions of production and sustenance. The history of sociology confirms the longevity of this range and may even suggest that limits to the basic form of that pluralism are cognitively fixed and socially variable only within these limits.[64] Of course variations in the extent and character of the institutionalization of sociology will affect sociological pluralism but although the mixture may vary the ingredients look much the same. Whether this is due to the naturally limited range of meta-theoretical positions or not is open to conjecture. But we do seem continually to bump our noses against the same issues within the same 'theoretical space'.[65] There is a special and inevitable pluralism in social science compared with natural science. We apprehend this pluralism often as muddle or pathological disunity and we index it notably in the diversity of meanings accorded to basic terms which all sociologists use.[66] Sociologists must constitute their object world. It does not have the fixity or tenability of the natural world and this is done by the use of basic theories and more particularly by the invention of concepts and the demonstration of their use by providing examples. It is not just a case, in sociology, of the absence of a neutral observational language; it is the fact that language must constitute the phenomena often taken, erroneously, to be constitutive of the discipline. That is, in effect, that language constitutes the discipline.

The particular pluralism which must stem from the centrality of language in the social disciplines is complicated and extended by the very diffuseness of disciplinary identification and what I can only clumsily call 'knowledge production' which has followed from sociology's peculiar institutional history. It is primarily the housing of sociology in university departments which has permitted the co-existence of a variety of approaches and a range of role-referents for sociologists.[67] Organizational settings have allowed and even encouraged variable patterns of pluralism. This has sometimes meant 'extension' and sometimes 'fission' but such styles of pluralism are the organizational forms of the raw materials of meta-theoretical agendas.[68] As Worsley notes, all major ideologies, even the apparently absolutist ones, are pluralist.[69] As he says 'Intellectual systems are inherently complex bodies of thought whose systematicity is always problematic: they can be decomposed, recomposed, added to, modified, have bits cut off and so on.' The implication is that a monism or absolutist conception of sociology, a 'true' sociology to be found somewhere in the midst of factional infighting, requires a mistaken view of the discipline.

None the less this does not imply that we must abandon judgment between competing views of society. If pluralism is inevitable we make our judgments on extra-disciplinary grounds as I have already suggested. More pertinently we must judge not what is an appropriate kind of sociology but we must learn to judge what is of no use to us in our extra-disciplinary aims and what we can dispense with.

This fairly abstract discussion of pluralism will perhaps become more vivid through a discussion of the confrontations between rival schools of sociology. Such antagonisms as were generated by sociological pluralism sadly hampered the growth of sociology in the period roughly from the late 1960s to the mid 1970s. There are signs that such fruitless conflict is now at an end and a new more tolerant mode of pluralism is reasserting itself.

Schism and fragmentation in sociology

It became accepted at the period of the height of sociology's popularity, both as a method of teaching sociology and as a way of claiming a cosy allegiance by the researcher in a hostile environment to appeal to a particular tradition, style or mode within sociology rather than to the discipline itself. It was almost a *sine qua non* of sociological education that the student and practitioner should define himself oppositionally. The history of the subject was reconstructed as one of opposing traditions, for instance Marx versus Weber, and the biographies of contemporary sociologists were often read as conversions from one mode to another (X used to be a structural functionalist but he is now an Althusserian marxist or a Schutzian phenomenologist).

It is worth clarifying the nature of some of these choices, to unpack the apparent oppositions and to try to work towards some more useful criteria for theoretical choice than are conventionally and implicitly offered and taken up. In sociology courses what usually happened was that the student was presented with an inventory or 'shopping list' of theoretical topics each only tenuously related to any other but most appearing to be mutually exclusive. It seemed as if you had to be an X sociologist and being X precluded and even condemned Y. Theories prescribe certain beliefs and attitudes, permit certain variations and proscribe others. But we rarely made such choices themselves the topic of theoretical consideration. Topics such as the nature of recurrent and unresolvable tensions within social science as a whole and the nature of dichotomous social thinking are rare.

How do we read the apparent oppositions? As historical reactions and re-reactions in a narrative of the discipline? We can be more reflexive than this. We can heuristically conceive of four conditioning bases of theoretical choice:[70] (a) the political: political movements are themselves defined oppositionally; (b) the practical: tasks have to be performed, goals defined, problems solved and the limits to these are set within organizations; (c) the theoretical: internal, formal requirements for the sake, perhaps, of consistence or coherence; (d) the cultural: wider currents of values styles, affiliations, fashions which act to demarcate group memberships. This is only one way of looking at the field. Gouldner's 'technical/formal' and 'infrastructural' levels is another.[71] But these are possible criteria for demarcating social theorizing. Some theorists explicitly appeal to a particular basis. For instance phenomenologists appeal to an explicit theoretical base and it unfortunately became conventional to criticize an opponent's theory by reference to its political or cultural base – varieties of *ad hominem* argument in the end. Attempts to explain away sociological styles by political or cultural allegiance are not particularly helpful. What is worth noting however is that these bases led sociologists only as far as rival versions of Bernstein's 'approach paradigms', never to fully-fledged rival explanations. To compete at the level of such approach paradigms requiring discussion about, for instance, the model of man assumed, easily led to heresy hunting and witch spotting. Sociologists can argue seemingly *ad infinitum* and without ever talking about social events beyond their own arguments, about what view of social phenomena sociologists ought to have. Explanations produced will be weak and non-comparable because they are approach-specific.

Consider the following sets of oppositions; 'classical versus romantic'; 'formalist versus substantive'; 'normative versus interpretive'; 'system versus action'; 'orthodox versus radical'; 'humanist versus positivist'.[72] All these dichotomies are examples of contemporary attempts to characterize the important distinctions between types of sociology. Most of them employed different criteria (for instance, methodological, stylistic, moral) but they managed to come up with distinct bifurcations in the history and practice of sociological theory. You can adhere to one type or the other but not to both.[73]

Can we trace some regularities in these oppositions. It is possible to separate what we have already called in chapter one 'orthodox' and 'radical'. Over the period roughly 1967 to 1975, due partly to the activities of such sociologists of sociology as those quoted above, combined with the rise of the New Left in the late 1960s and the populist appeal of anti-determinist theories, especially of deviance, such false opposite positions came to have canonical status. They were accepted and sociologists, especially students, came to define themselves in terms of them. Broadly what we saw was an opposition between scholarship (which was believed to be value-neutral and concerned with explanation) and a loose 'field of study' (value-committed and concerned with activism, criticism and exposure). Many of the debates in academic sociological theory were about four things: objectivism, prediction, determinism and value-neutrality. Partisanship spread accordingly. Simple dichotomies of the radical versus orthodox type are misleading as alliances but they complicated sociological life unmercifully.

There is no consensus in the discipline. There is precious little articulate disagreement either. As Gibbs has said, sociologists write for a clique and no publication is likely to reach more than about one quarter of one's nominal colleagues.[74] The problem is how best can we categorize the variety of theory in a discipline which is in a state of fragmentation and where existing popular divisions merely reinforce muddled allegiances? The question following on from that is how do we reconcile different approaches? Explicit reference to some end towards which theory is a means is one way. The selection of criteria intrinsic to theory itself is the other. A choice has to be made. Explaining these two methods of assessing theory is a major task within sociology theory. It involves examining the links between theory and action in each case and making open statements about the relation between the sociologist as philosopher and the sociologist as concerned with social intervention. The question of the reconciliation of differences is both a theoretical and a disciplinary matter. Do we advocate struggle, eclecticism, attempts to make apparent differences compatible in strategic terms or what?

Modes of pluralism

The commonest recent method of sociologists coping with the pluralism of their subject is by trying to submerge it in a debate about 'paradigms'. The term came into prominent use following the popularity of Kuhn's analysis of scientific change[75] and several descriptions of sociology's diverse appearance use the paradigm concept.[76] The term itself has no clear and agreed meaning,[77] but it has been largely used in the sense of a tradition of scientific work which has adherents and exemplary achievements sufficient to grant it social orthodoxy. Kuhn suggested that natural science progressed by revolutionary change from paradigm to paradigm. The use made of this notion with respect to sociology was to suggest that sociology as a discipline was either pre-paradigmatic or multi-paradigmatic and in general the concept was used as a formal means of debating disciplinary pluralism.[78] As Giddens suggests, similar notions of discontinuous and often competing 'frames of reference' have been suggested from divergent philosophical traditions.[79]

In general the paradigm debate in sociology has been disappointing in that it has been more concerned either to compare the social disciplines with Kuhn's description of, for instance, physics, or it has been preoccupied with the discontinuities between traditions of thought and enquiry which themselves claim the mantle of the one true sociology. Giddens notes that it is necessarily true that paradigms *must* to some extent be continuous, else how can we learn to operate and operate in a new paradigm?[80]

Thus discussion which stresses 'epistemological breaks' and revolutions can neither cope with the continuousness of change (even within situations within which people believe a radical rupture to have occurred) nor can they illuminate the variety which is itself the structure of a discipline rather than its aberration. Paradigm discussions have assumed cut-off points between theories and the desirability, even if implicit, of an overriding theory.

What are the alternative strategies of coping with and exploiting pluralism in sociology? We can see three broad approaches. First, there is the 'open warfare' approach or the view that competition should be encouraged. This maximizes the apparent discontinuity between theories and in the end is a recipe for increasing schism, fragmentation and internecine strife and the abandonment of a purpose for sociology beyond the fighting of its own internal battles. Second, there is the approach which holds to a 'natural' progress towards a unified and absolute kind of sociology and which sees contemporary diversity as a symptom only of immaturity which will be inevitably corrected in time. Thus, while we must endure the lurches and staggers of fashion, there is an undercurrent of progress and maturity to sociological thought. The third position is a more complicated one and is concerned with the mode of co-existence of a number of theories within a wider discipline. Two recent but very different accounts help to clarify this mode of co-existence.

Eisenstadt and Curelaru discuss two approaches seen in sociological writings.[81] First, the 'constructive' approach which accepts some surrounding agreed concern with a distinctive sociological tradition. Within this perimeter consensus a range of analysis and research is permissible and tension and mutual criticism can be supported. Second, the 'abdicative' approach which depends upon the abandonment of the conviction that cognitive scientific objectivity of any kind is possible and the submission of sociological thought to aesthetic or ideological criteria or to some notion of a transcendent activism. The difficulty implicit in this account is that a constructive approach to pluralism requires some degree of *a priori* or at least pre-committed disciplinary consensus. This may be at a much more generalized level than is conventionally assumed when pessimistic critics of sociology bewail its lack of a natural consensus. It may be quite adequately exemplified in the belief that the institutional existence of social science should not wither away and that disciplined dialogue about sociological matters should continue. Within such a boundary pluralism of the kind we now see can flourish. Yet this is simply a prescription for the organizational requirements of co-existence.

At a more personal level the recent posthumously published work of Halmos points us towards the more profound conditions for sociological pluralism and co-existence.[82] His concern with 'equilibration' and the straightforward view that 'the holding of incompatible positions is integral to sociological thinking'[83] amounts to the most eloquent manifesto yet for co-existence. He warns us to beware of mergers, fusions, syntheses and compromises as the verbal smotherings of pluralism, and of transcendencies and dialectics as its rhetorical avoidance. Paradox and contradiction are qualities of life and must be borne, not talked away. We must learn to live with differences. This must be the deep structure of pluralism and the moral basis of an interventionist sociology.

Notes

Chapter 1 Sociology's place

1 P. Abrams, *The Origins of British Sociology, 1834–1914*, Harmondsworth, Penguin, 1968.
2 B. Moore Jr, *Reflections on the Causes of Human Misery*, London, Allen Lane, 1972.
3 A. Gouldner, *For Sociology*, Harmondsworth, Penguin, 1975, especially chapter 3.
4 Ibid., p. 80.
5 R. Nisbet, *Sociology as an Art Form*, London, Heinemann, 1976. R. H. Brown, *A Poetic for Sociology*, Cambridge University Press, 1977.
6 This is especially true in the work of Max Weber: see for instance H. H. Gerth and C. W. Mills (eds), *From Max Weber*, London, Routledge & Kegan Paul, 1948, especially chapter V, 'Science as a Vocation'.
7 The growth of institutional sociology has been recent and rapid. Heraud notes the number of chairs of sociology rising from three to twenty between 1962 and 1964! B. J. Heraud, *Sociology and Social Work: Perspectives and Problems*, Oxford, Pergamon, 1970, p. 13.
8 See for instance J. H. Turner, *The Structure of Sociological Theory*, Homewood, Ill., Dorsey, 1974, for a criticism of the game of 'criticizing the discipline'.
9 See J. Bailey, *Social Theory for Planning*, London, Routledge & Kegan Paul, 1975, chapter 1.
10 See D. J. Manning, *Liberalism*, London, Dent, 1976, chapter 6.
11 B. Fay, *Social Theory and Political Practice*, London, Allen & Unwin, 1975, is one of the best descriptions of the relation.
12 See P. M. Worsley, 'The State of Theory and the Status of Theory', *Sociology*, 8, 1974, pp. 1–17.
13 See A. R. Louch, *Explanation and Human Action*, Oxford, Blackwell, 1966.
14 Fay, op. cit., chapter 2.
15 See for instance J. Meynaud, *Technocracy*, London, Faber, 1968.
16 The resonance of the concept of 'paradigm' in discussions of the condition of sociological theory is notable, especially given the difficulties and perhaps the inappropriateness of the foundation text, T. S. Kuhn, *The Structure of*

Scientific Revolutions, University of Chicago Press, 1962. For a brief but incisive discussion of the implications of the concept for judging the condition of academic sociology see C. G. A. Bryant, 'Kuhn, Paradigms and Sociology', *British Journal of Sociology*, 26, 1975, pp. 354–9.

17 For instance P. N. Nidditch (ed.), *The Philosophy of Science*, London, Oxford University Press, 1968.

18 T. W. Adorno *et al.*, *The Positivist Dispute in German Sociology*, London, Heinemann, 1976.

19 This is most evident in the work of L. Althusser, especially in his *For Marx*, London, Allen Lane, 1969, and *Lenin and Philosophy and Other Essays*, London, New Left Books, 1971.

20 For instance N. W. Storer, *The Social System of Science*, New York, Holt, Rinehart & Winston, 1966.

21 See for this term J. Agassi, 'Scientific Problems and their Roots in Metaphysics', in M. Bunge (ed.), *The Critical Approach to Science and Philosophy*, Cambridge, Mass., Harvard University Press, 1964.

22 Kuhn, op. cit.

23 See L. I. Krimerman (ed.), *The Nature and Scope of the Social Sciences*, New York, Appleton, 1969, for an example of how these values are taken to be iconic for the social disciplines.

24 This of course refers to the work of Karl Popper, *The Logic of Scientific Discovery*, London, Hutchinson, 1968; *Conjectures and Refutations*, London, Routledge & Kegan Paul, 1969; also see E. Nagel, *The Structure of Science*, London, Routledge & Kegan Paul, 1961.

25 For an early and perhaps crude statement of this possibility see J. D. Bernal, *The Social Function of Science*, London, George Routledge, 1939.

26 H. and S. Rose (eds), *The Political Economy of Science*, London, Macmillan, 1976.

27 H. Marcuse, *One-Dimensional Man*, London, Sphere, 1968, p. 121.

28 In J. Habermas, *Toward a Rational Society*, London, Heinemann, 1970.

29 See B. Barnes (ed.), *Sociology of Science*, Harmondsworth, Penguin, 1972, Part 3; and many of the contributions to J. D. Douglas (ed.), *Freedom and Tyranny: Some Problems of a Technological Society*, New York, Knopf, 1970.

30 Rose and Rose (eds), op. cit., chapter 2.

31 For instance J. Ellul, *The Technical Society*, London, Cape, 1965; Meynaud, op. cit.

32 For instance S. Box and S. Cotgrove, *Science, Industry and Society*, London, Allen & Unwin, 1970.

33 R. K. Merton, *Social Theory and Social Structure*, New York, Free Press, 1968, Part IV.

34 For a penetrating criticism of Habermas on this point see H. Albert, 'The Myth of Total Reason', in A. Giddens (ed.), *Positivism and Sociology*, London, Heinemann, 1974.

35 Nisbet, op. cit; Brown, op. cit.

36 J. H. Plumb (ed.), *Crisis in the Humanities*, Harmondsworth, Penguin, 1964.

37 E. Gellner, 'The Crisis in the Humanities and the Mainstream of Philosophy', in Plumb, op. cit.

38 Powerfully put in D. Bell, *The Cultural Contradictions of Capitalism*, London, Heinemann, 1976.

39 Most famously seen in M. Arnold, *Culture and Anarchy*, Cambridge University Press, 1969 (1869).

40 The interest in the importance of culture can be seen in a 'traditional' form in for instance E. Goodhart, *Culture and the Radical Conscience*, Cambridge, Mass., Harvard University Press, 1973; and famously in L. Trilling, *Sincerity and Authenticity*, London, Oxford University Press, 1972. In a more sociological, analytical sense see P. Willis, *Profane Culture*, London, Routledge & Kegan Paul, 1978; R. Sennett, *The Fall of Public Man*, Cambridge University Press, 1976; Z. Bauman, *Culture as Praxis*, London, Routledge & Kegan Paul, 1973.

41 For a readable account of hermeneutics see A. Giddens, *New Rules of Sociological Method*, London, Hutchinson, 1976, especially pp. 54–70.

42 I. A. Richards, *Principles of Literary Criticism*, London, Routledge & Kegan Paul, 1960 (1924), p. 211.

43 See M. Bulmer, 'The Prospects for Applied Sociology', *British Journal of Sociology*, 29, 1978, pp. 128–35.

44 Notably A. W. Gouldner and S. M. Miller (eds), *Applied Sociology : Opportunities and Problems*, New York, Free Press, 1966; A. B. Shostak (ed.), *Sociology in Action : Case Studies in Social Problems and Applied Social Change*, Homewood, Ill., Dorsey, 1966; P. F. Lazarsfeld, W. H. Sewell and H. C. Wilensky (eds), *The Uses of Sociology*, New York, Basic Books, 1967. For a less than critical commentary see H. Waitzkin, 'Truth's Search for Power: The Dilemma of the Social Sciences', in J. D. Douglas (ed.), *The Relevance of Sociology*, New York, Appleton-Century-Crofts, 1970.

45 See especially H. L. Zetterberg, *Social Theory and Social Practice*, New York, Bedminster Press, 1962.

46 See for instance C. Argyris and D. Schön, *Theory in Practice, Increasing Professional Effectiveness*, California, Jossey-Bass, 1974; A. Podgorecki, *Practical Social Sciences*, London, Routledge & Kegan Paul, 1975.

47 See R. Pinker, *Social Theory and Social Policy*, London, Heinemann, 1971; J. Madge, *The Tools of Social Science*, London, Longman, 1953.

48 Bryant, op. cit.

49 For instance A. W. Gouldner, *The Coming Crisis of Western Sociology*, London, Heinemann, 1971.

50 As, for instance, was R. Aron, *Main Currents in Sociological Thought*, Harmondsworth, Penguin, 2 vols, 1965, 1968.

51 M. Glucksmann, *Structuralist Analysis in Contemporary Sociological Thought*, London, Routledge & Kegan Paul, 1974, pp. 9–10.

52 For instance S. Mennell, *Sociological Theory : Uses and Unities*, London, Nelson, 1974.

53 N. Rescher, *The Primacy of Practice*, Oxford, Blackwell, 1973.

54 For instance R. Fletcher's hymn to evolutionism, 'Evolutionary and Developmental Sociology', in J. Rex (ed.), *Approaches to Sociology*, London, Routledge & Kegan Paul, 1974.

55 S. Cohen says in addressing social workers: 'Tell those sociologists who urge you to be theoretically sophisticated to get off your backs. (They are the same sociologists who want to turn their own subject into matters of epistemology and philosophy.)' S. Cohen, 'It's Alright for You to Talk: Political and Sociological Manifestos for Social Work Action', in R. Bailey and M. Brake (eds), *Radical Social Work*, London, Arnold, 1975, p. 94.

56 For instance see C. Cockburn's discussion of sociologists' and others' promotion of the concept of 'community' in the context of the state's view of 'urban problems', C. Cockburn, *The Local State : Management of Cities and People*, London, Pluto Press, 1977, chapter 4.

Chapter 2   Disciplines and professions

1 The problem is one of relativism. Simply put, what is the status of statements produced by a sociology of knowledge which attempts to relate knowledge to society? See N. Elias, 'Sociology of Knowledge: New Perspectives', Parts One and Two, *Sociology*, 5, 1974, pp. 149–68, 335–70; P. Hamilton, *Knowledge and Social Structure*, London, Routledge & Kegan Paul, 1974.

2 See E. Freidson, 'Professionalization and the Organization of Middle Class Labour in Post-Industrial Society', in P. Halmos (ed.), *Sociological Review Monograph*, no. 20, University of Keele, 1973, p. 50.

3 As does Freidson, ibid., and D. Bell, *The Coming of Post-Industrial Society*, Harmondsworth, Peregrine, 1974.

4 As most marxists do. For instance, N. Poulantzas, *Classes in Contemporary Capitalism*, London, New Left Books, 1975; G. Carchedi, 'On the Economic Identification of the New Middle Class', *Economy and Society*, 4, 1975, pp. 1–86.

5 How far this is true of even the 'formal' disciplines is problematic. For mathematics for instance see D. Struik, *A Concise History of Mathematics*, New York, Dover, 1976; B. Lumpkin, 'History of Mathematics in the Age of Imperialism', *Science and Society*, XLII, 1978, pp. 178–84.

6 See C. G. A. Bryant, 'Kuhn, Paradigms and Sociology', *British Journal of Sociology*, 26, 1975, pp. 354–9.

7 For instance Hayek has described how the separate functions of the École Polytechnique and the Collège de France in the eighteenth century fathered the major intellectual developments of the nineteenth century – scientism and socialism – through commitments to engineering and ideology respectively. See F. Hayek, 'Scientism and the Study of Society', in J. O'Neill (ed.), *Modes of Individualism and Collectivism*, London, Heinemann, 1973.

8 L. Althusser, *For Marx*, London, Allen Lane, 1969.

9 G. Therborn, *Science, Class and Society*, London, New Left Books, 1976.

10 Ibid., pp. 69–70.

11 See for instance M. Castells, 'Theory and Ideology in Urban Sociology', in C. G. Pickvance (ed.), *Urban Sociology: Critical Essays*, London, Tavistock, 1976, p. 60.

12 Therborn, op. cit., p. 71.

13 Also see D. Willer and J. Willer, *Systematic Empiricism: A Critique of Pseudo-Science*, Englewood Cliffs, NJ, Prentice-Hall, 1976; B. Hindess, *The Use of Official Statistics in Sociology*, London, Routledge & Kegan Paul, 1973; and the exchange between Hindess and Pickvance in *Economy and Society*, 2, 1973, following B. Hindess, 'Models and masks: Empiricist conceptions of the conditions of scientific knowledge', *Economy and Society*, 2, 1973, pp. 233–44. Therborn himself dismisses taxonomy as a viable scientific enterprise a little too cavalierly, op. cit., p. 70.

14 Therborn, op. cit., p. 143.

15 S. N. Eisenstadt and M. Curelaru, *The Form of Sociology: Paradigms and Crises*, New York, Wiley, 1976.

16 See for example J. Ben-David and A. Zloczower, 'Universities and Academic Systems in Modern Societies', *Archives Européennes de Sociologie*, 3, 1962, pp. 45–84.

17 A. W. Gouldner, *The Coming Crisis of Western Sociology*, London, Heinemann, 1971, pp. 36–8.

18 Ibid., p. 170.

19 J. Ben-David and R. Collins, 'Social Factors in the Origins of a New Science: The Case of Psychology', *American Sociological Review*, 31, 1966, pp. 451–65.

20 For a general view see Halmos (ed.), op. cit.

21 See A. Etzioni, *The Semi-Professions and their Organization*, London, Collier Macmillan, 1969.

22 For instance see J. A. Jackson (ed.), *Professions and Professionalization*, Cambridge University Press, 1972, p. 3.

23 See T. J. Johnson, *Professions and Power*, London, Heinemann, 1972. This is the most powerful analytical approach to professions readily available.

24 Ibid., chapter 1.

25 Johnson especially, but also see E. Freidson, *Professional Dominance*, New York, Dodd, Mead, 1972; N. Oppenheimer, 'The Proletarianization of the Professional', in Halmos (ed.), op. cit.

26 On the importance of the concept of 'closure' see F. Parkin, 'Strategies of Social Closure in Class Formation', in Parkin (ed.), *The Social Analysis of Class Structure*, London, Tavistock/BSA, 1974.

27 T. J. Johnson, 'The Professions in the Class Structure', in R. Scase (ed.), *Industrial Society: Class, Cleavage and Control*, London, Allen & Unwin, 1977.

28 For an example of this in the medical field (where it is more obvious and dramatic than in other areas) see G. Larkin, 'Medical Dominance and

Control: Radiographers in the Division of Labour', *Sociological Review*, 26, 1978.

29 H. Jamous and B. Peloille, 'Professions or Self-Perpetuating Systems: Changes in the French University-Hospital System', in Jackson (ed.), op. cit.

30 Johnson, 1977, op. cit.

31 Jamous and Peloille, op. cit., p. 112.

32 Johnson, 1977, op. cit. He relies for this approach on G. Carchedi, op. cit. Also see G. Carchedi, 'Reproduction of social classes at the level of production relations', *Economy and Society*, 4, 1975, pp. 361–417.

33 Jackson's protests to the contrary, see note 22.

34 For instance W. G. Runciman, *Sociology in its Place*, Cambridge University Press, 1970.

35 See G. Benveniste, *The Politics of Expertise*, London, Croom Helm, 1973.

36 I. Gerver and J. Bensman, 'Towards a Sociology of Expertness', *Social Forces*, 1953–4, 22, pp. 226–35. The idea of 'expertise' is a central though complicated one not least because, as Giddens notes, 'expertise in the world of social relations is not incidental to social life but is the very medium of its orderliness. The necessary intersubjectivity of the social world makes it "our world" in a way that has no parallel in the relations of human beings to nature where knowledge is certainly routinely used in a transformative way but where that knowledge is not part of the conditions of existence of the universe of objects and events to which it relates.' A. Giddens, *Studies in Social and Political Theory*, London, Hutchinson, 1977, p. 27.

37 See B. Fay, *Social Theory and Political Practice*, London, Allen & Unwin, 1975, chapters 2 and 3.

38 K. Mannheim, *Ideology and Utopia*, London, Routledge & Kegan Paul, 1960 (1936), pp. 136–46.

39 For instance E. Shils, *The Intellectuals and the Powers and Other Essays*, University of Chicago Press, 1972.

40 Ibid., p. 9.

41 A. Gramsci, *Collected Works*, vol. 4, *Gli Intellettuale e l'organizzazione della cultura*, Turin, Einaudi, 1949. Accessible accounts of Gramsci's discussion of intellectuals are in A. Pozzolini, *Antonio Gramsci: An Introduction to his Thought*, London, Pluto Press, 1977; J. Joll, *Gramsci*, London, Fontana, 1977; J. Cammett, *Antonio Gramsci and the Origins of Italian Communism*, California, Stanford University Press, 1967.

Chapter 3   Law and social theory

1 J. Rex (ed.), *Sociology and the Demystification of the Modern World*, London, Routledge & Kegan Paul, 1974, p. 22.

2 See N. Harding, *Lenin's Political Thought*, London, Macmillan, 1977, chapter 9, 'Theory and Practice in the Democratic Revolution', for an influential statement of this view.

3 For instance M. Shaw, 'The Coming Crisis of Radical Sociology', in R. Blackburn (ed.), *Ideology in Social Science*, London, Fontana, 1972.

4 I. Taylor, P. Walton and J. Young, *The New Criminology*, London, Routledge & Kegan Paul, 1973, chapter 6, provide this comparable dismissal.

5 P. Rock, *Deviant Behaviour*, London, Hutchinson, 1973, chapter 3, provides a sensitive description of the importance of law, especially pp. 122–32.

6 See for example R. M. Unger, *Law in Modern Society*, New York, Free Press, 1976.

7 Durkheim is the best known example of this approach. E. Durkheim, *The Division of Labour in Society*, New York, Free Press, 1964.

8 J. N. Shklar, *Legalism: An Essay on Law, Morals and Politics*, Cambridge, Mass., Harvard University Press, 1964.

9 J. Gibbs, 'The Sociology of Law and Normative Phenomena', *American Sociological Review*, 31, 1966, pp. 315–25, makes this argument explicit.

10 For example P. Carlen, 'Remedial Routines for the Maintenance of Control in Magistrates' Courts', *British Journal of Law and Society*, 1, 1974, pp. 107–17.

11 J. Hall, *Studies in Jurisprudence and Criminal Theory*, New York, Oceana Publications, 1958; W. Twining, 'Some Jobs for Jurisprudence', *British Journal of Law and Society*, 1, 1974, pp. 149–74.

12 See J. Stone, *The Province and Function of Law*, Sydney, Maitland, 1950.

13 For examples of such impositions see N. F. Timasheff, 'The Growth and Scope of the Sociology of Law', in H. Becker and A. Boskoff, *Modern Sociological Theory in Continuity and Change*, New York, Holt, Rhinehart & Winston, 1957; G. Gurvitch, *The Sociology of Law*, London, Routledge & Kegan Paul, 1947; Stone, op. cit.; J. Hall, *Comparative Law and Social Theory*, Baton Rouge, Louisiana State University Press, 1963; P. Brett, *An Essay in Contemporary Jurisprudence*, London, Butterworth, 1975.

14 Twining, op. cit.; C. Campbell, 'Legal Thought and Juristic Values', *British Journal of Law and Society*, 1, 1974, pp. 13–30; D. N. Schiff, 'Socio-Legal Theory: Social Structure and Law', *Modern Law Review*, 39, 1976, pp. 282–310.

15 J. Stone, *Law and the Social Sciences*, Minneapolis, University of Minnesota Press, 1966, pp. 4–5.

16 J. Austin, *Lectures on Jurisprudence and the Philosophy of Positive Law*, London, Murray, 1885.

17 W. H. Hohfeld, *Fundamental Legal Conceptions as Applied in Judicial Reasoning*, New Haven, Yale University Press, 1966 (1919).

18 H. Kelsen, *General Theory of Law and State*, Berkeley, University of California Press, 1945.

19 Gurvitch, op. cit., p. 7.

20 'Legal realism' could only avoid this by abandoning theory as such altogether: see for instance W. Twining, *Karl Llewellyn and the Realist Movement*, London, Weidenfeld & Nicolson, 1973.

21 Campbell, op. cit., who relies heavily upon V. Aubert, 'Researches in the Sociology of Law', *American Behavioral Scientist*, 7, 1963, pp. 16–20.

22 Ibid., pp. 13–14. Campbell relies here on C. Perelman, *The Idea of Justice and the Problem of Argument*, London, Routledge & Kegan Paul, 1963.

23 T. Eckhoff and N. K. Sundby, 'The Notion of Basic Norm(s) in Jurisprudence', *Scandinavian Studies in Law*, 19, Stockholm, Almqvist and Wiksell, 1975.

24 Campbell, op. cit.

25 Schiff, op. cit., p. 309.

26 Gibbs, op. cit.

27 See note 1, chapter 2; and J. Bailey, *Social Theory for Planning*, London, Routledge & Kegan Paul, 1975, chapter 2.

28 T. Midgley, 'The Role of Legal History', *British Journal of Law and Society*, 2, 1975, pp. 153–65, p. 155.

29 Hall, 1963, op. cit., p. 30.

30 Twining, 'Some Jobs for Jurisprudence', p. 160.

31 For instance nearly all the contributors to R. M. Dworkin (ed.), *The Philosophy of Law*, London, Oxford University Press, 1977.

32 Midgley, op. cit.

33 See V Aubert, op. cit.

34 For a less pessimistic view see R. Treves, 'Co-operation between Lawyers and Sociologists: A Comparative Comment', *British Journal of Law and Society*, 1, 1974, pp. 200–4.

35 For instance see *American Behavioral Scientist*, Vol. 13, 4, 1970, issue on 'Law and Social Change'.

36 See for instance M. Shapiro, 'Political Jurisprudence', in R. J. Simon (ed.), *The Sociology of Law*, San Francisco, Chandler, 1968.

37 A. Goldstein, 'The Unfulfilled Promise of Legal Education', in S. Hazard (ed.), *Law in a Changing America*, Englewood Cliffs, NJ, Prentice-Hall, 1968.

38 A. Hunt, *The Sociological Movement in Law*, London, Macmillan, 1978, chapter 5.

39 Ibid., chapter 4. M. Clarke, 'Durkheim's Sociology of Law', *British Journal of Law and Society*, 3, 1976, pp. 246–55.

40 M. Cain, 'The Main Themes of Marx' and Engels' Sociology of Law', *British Journal of Law and Society*, 1, 1974, pp. 146–8.

41 A. Podgorecki *et al.*, *Knowledge and Opinion about Law*, London, Martin Robertson, 1973.

42 For an example of this see the furore surrounding the research and publication of M. McConville and J. Baldwin, *Negotiated Justice : Pressures to Plead Guilty*, London, Martin Robertson, 1977. See the *Sunday Times*, 18 September 1977, p. 14.

43 For instance A. K. Cohen, *Deviance and Control*, Englewood Cliffs, NJ, Prentice-Hall, 1966; D. Matza, *Becoming Deviant*, Englewood Cliffs, NJ, Prentice-Hall, 1969; Taylor, Walton and Young, op. cit.

44 For instance S. Cohen, 'Criminology and the Sociology of Deviance in Britain', in P. Rock and M. McIntosh (eds), *Deviance and Social Control*, London, Tavistock, 1974.

45 Matza, op. cit.

46 See particularly H. and J. Schwendinger, 'Defenders of order or guardians of human rights?', in I. Taylor, P. Walton and J. Young (eds), *Critical Criminology*, London, Routledge & Kegan Paul, 1975, as well as other papers in this volume.

47 Excluding S. Cohen, 1974, op. cit.

48 See Gouldner's similar description of the 'fit' of functionalism in general. A. W. Gouldner, *The Coming Crisis of Western Sociology*, London, Heinemann, 1971, pp. 341–50.

49 See Taylor, Walton and Young, 1975, op. cit., pp. 14–20, for a description of 'anti-utilitarian' criminology.

50 A recent example of this resistance is T. Morris, *Deviance and Control*, London, Hutchinson, 1976.

51 Bailey, op. cit., chapter 5.

52 This is an almost purely descriptive approach to the constitutional machinery of the state. See, for instance, W. Ivor Jennings, *The British Constitution*, Cambridge University Press, 1961; A. H. Birch, *Representative and Responsible Government*, London, Allen & Unwin, 1964.

53 See for example R. Collins, *Conflict Sociology*, New York, Academic Press, 1975; D. Binns, *Beyond the Sociology of Conflict*, London, Macmillan, 1977.

54 L. McDonald, *The Sociology of Law and Order*, London, Faber & Faber, 1976, provides a readable history.

55 T. Parsons, 'The Law and Social Control', in W. M. Evan (ed.), *Law and Sociology*, New York, Free Press, 1962.

56 P. Sorokin, *Social and Cultural Dynamics*, New York, American Books, 1937, vol. 2.

57 N. F. Timasheff, op. cit., 1957.

58 See Hunt, op. cit., chapter 4.

59 For a full exposition of this principle see W. J. Chambliss and R. B. Seidman, *Law, Order and Power*, Reading, Mass., Addison-Wesley, 1971.

60 Ibid., p. 201.

61 Binns, op. cit.

62 Ibid., p. 209.

63 See for instance R. Quinney, *The Social Reality of Crime*, Boston, Little Brown, 1970.

64 For instance E. P. Thompson, *Whigs and Hunters: The Origin of the Black Act*, London, Allen Lane, 1975; J. N. J. Palmer, 'Evils Merely Prohibited', *British Journal of Law and Society*, 3, 1976, pp. 1–16; M. C. Kennedy, 'Beyond Incrimination', *Catalyst*, 5, 1970, pp. 1–37.

65 Cain, op. cit.

66 K. Renner, *The Institutions of Private Law and their Social Functions*,

London, Routledge & Kegan Paul, 1949. Also see J. R. Commons, *The Legal Foundations of Capitalism*, Madison, University of Wisconsin Press, 1959.

67 For instance T. Duster, *The Legislation of Morality*, New York, Free Press, 1970 (on narcotics law); J. Gusfield, *Symbolic Crusade : Status Politics and the Temperance Movement*, Urbana, University of Illinois Press, 1963; A. M. Platt, *The Child Savers : The Invention of Delinquency*, University of Chicago Press, 1969.

68 Z. Bankowski and G. Mungham, *Images of Law*, London, Routledge & Kegan Paul, 1976, is the most muscular recent version.

69 See the Ormrod Report, *Report of the Committee on Legal Education*, Cmnd 4595, HMSO, 1971.

70 Bankowski and Mungham, op. cit., might think that this should be its object but are clear that 'socio-legal' studies are inadequate.

71 J. T. Winkler, 'Law, State, and Economy: The Industry Act 1975 in Context', *British Journal of Law and Society*, 2, 1975, pp. 103–28.

72 For an interesting introduction to this issue see G. Hawthorn, *Enlightenment and Despair*, Cambridge University Press, 1976, conclusion.

73 Especially recently in J. Rawls, *A Theory of Justice*, Oxford, Clarendon Press, 1972.

74 See N. P. Mouzelis, *Organization and Bureaucracy*, London, Routledge & Kegan Paul, 1967, pp. 15–26, for Weber's position.

75 Hunt, op. cit., chapter 4 and Clarke, op. cit., both summarize Durkheim's position.

76 B. Fay, *Social Theory and Political Practice*, London, Allen & Unwin, 1975, chapter 1, describes the applicability of the theory of social science as 'engineering'.

77 J. O'Neill (ed.), *Modes of Individualism and Collectivism*, London, Heinemann, 1973, p. 15.

78 K. Popper, *The Poverty of Historicism*, London, Routledge & Kegan Paul, 1957; *The Open Society and its Enemies*, London, Routledge & Kegan Paul, 1966.

79 F. A. Hayek, *The Road to Serfdom*, London, Routledge & Kegan Paul, 1962; *Studies in Philosophy, Politics and Economics*, London, Routledge & Kegan Paul, 1967; *Individualism and Economic Order*, London, Routledge & Kegan Paul, 1976 (1949).

80 A. Giddens, *New Rules of Sociological Method*, London, Hutchinson, 1976.

81 W. G. Runciman, *Sociology in its Place and Other Essays*, Cambridge University Press, 1970.

82 See for instance C. B. McPherson, *The Political Theory of Possessive Individualism*, Oxford, Clarendon Press, 1962.

83 Notably in F. A. Hayek, *Law, Legislation and Liberty*, London, Routledge & Kegan Paul, 3 vols, 1973–8.

84 Ibid., vol. 1, p. 123.

85 Rawls, op. cit.

86 See for instance R. Miller, 'Rawls and Marxism', and M. Fisk, 'History and Reason in Rawls' Moral Theory', in N. Daniels (ed.), *Reading Rawls*, Oxford, Blackwell, 1975; B. Barry, *The Liberal Theory of Justice*, Oxford, Clarendon Press, 1973.

87 For instance J. Floud, 'Sociology and the Theory of Responsibility', in R. Fletcher (ed.), *The Science of Society and the Unity of Mankind*, London, Heinemann/BSA, 1974.

Chapter 4   Social work and social theory

1 See A. Podgorecki *et al.*, *Knowledge and Opinion about Law*, London, Martin Robertson, 1973.

2 For instance in R. Bailey and M. Brake (eds), *Radical Social Work*, London, Arnold, 1975, p. 1.

3 For a discussion of 'practical objects', 'theoretical objects' and 'scientific objects' in another interventionist context see M. Castells, 'Is there an urban sociology?', in C. G. Pickvance (ed.), *Urban Sociology : Critical Essays*, London, Tavistock, 1976.

4 See for instance R. Hamilton, 'Social Work: An Aspiring Profession and its Difficulties', *British Journal of Social Work*, 4, 1974, pp. 333–42; B. Sheldon, 'Theory and Practice in Social Work: An Examination of a Tenuous Relationship', *British Journal of Social Work*, 8, 1978, pp. 1–22.

5 See the Annual Abstracts of Data produced by the Central Council for Education and Training in Social Work. The number of social work courses has increased by about one third since 1972.

6 B. Jordan, *Freedom and the Welfare State*, London, Routledge & Kegan Paul, 1976, chapter 10.

7 For instance P. Halmos, *The Faith of the Counsellors*, London, Constable, 1965; *The Personal Service Society*, London, Constable, 1970; R. Titmuss, *The Gift Relationship*, London, Allen & Unwin, 1970.

8 Noted for instance by R. Evans, 'Some Implications of an Integrated Model of Social Work for Theory and Practice', *British Journal of Social Work*, 6, 1976, pp. 177–200, p. 179.

9 This is especially obviously true for occupational groups appealing to natural science as a knowledge base. The position is more complex in social-science-based occupations but is still true in principle.

10 For instance K. Woodroffe, *From Charity to Social Work*, London, Routledge & Kegan Paul, 1962.

11 See J. Bailey, *Social Theory for Planning*, London, Routledge & Kegan Paul, 1975, chapter 5.

12 P. Seed, *The Expansion of Social Work in Britain*, London, Routledge & Kegan Paul, 1973.

13 For instance Z. T. Butrym, *The Nature of Social Work*, London, Macmillan, 1976, chapter 9; Jordan, op. cit., p. 158.

14 For instance E. J. Thomas (ed.), *Behavioral Science for Social Workers*, New

York, Free Press, 1967, exemplifies the full, pretentious irrelevance of this approach.

15 See R. W. Roberts and R. H. Nee (eds), *Theories of Social Casework*, University of Chicago Press, 1970.

16 The bibles of this approach seem to be A. Pincus and A. Minahan, *Social Work Practice: Model and Method*, Itasca, Ill., Peacock, 1973; and H. Goldstein, *Social Work Practice: A Unitary Approach*, Columbia, University of South Carolina Press, 1973.

17 See the discussion of psychiatry in G. Pearson, *The Deviant Imagination: Psychiatry, Social Work and Social Change*, London, Macmillan, 1975, especially pp. 127–32; and, rather differently, in P. Halmos, *The Personal and the Political: Social Work and Political Action*, London, Hutchinson, 1978.

18 For instance G. Pearson, 'Making Social Workers: Bad Promises and Good Omens', and S. Cohen, 'It's Alright for You to Talk: Political and Sociological Manifestos for Social Work Action', both in Bailey and Brake (eds), op. cit.

19 See R. Deacon and M. Bartley, 'Becoming a Social Worker', in H. Jones (ed.), *Towards a New Social Work*, London, Routledge & Kegan Paul, 1975.

20 O. Stevenson, 'Knowledge for Social Work', *British Journal of Social Work*, 1, 1971, pp. 225–37, p. 226.

21 Butrym, op. cit., chapter 4.

22 Ibid., p. 14.

23 Ibid., p. x.

24 Evans, op. cit., p. 179.

25 For instance B. J. Heraud, *Sociology and Social Work: Perspectives and Problems*, Oxford, Pergamon, 1970.

26 H. M. Bartlett, *The Common Base of Social Work Practice*, New York, National Association of Social Workers, 1970.

27 Ibid., pp. 38, 47, 108–9.

28 R. E. Smalley, *Theory for Social Work Practice*, New York, Columbia University Press, 1967.

29 Ibid., p. 133, and chapter 8.

30 See M. Masterman, 'The Nature of a Paradigm', in I. Lakatos and A. Musgrave (eds), *Criticism and the Growth of Knowledge*, Cambridge University Press, 1970, for twenty-one different uses of the term 'paradigm' in one seminal work.

31 See for instance P. Leonard, 'Explanation and Education in Social Work', *British Journal of Social Work*, 5, 1975, pp. 325–33.

32 Seed, op. cit., Butrym, op. cit.

33 Bailey and Brake (eds), op. cit.

34 Butrym, op. cit., pp. 71–3.

35 See for instance Heraud, op. cit., pp. 40–3.

36 Ibid.; P. Leonard, *Sociology in Social Work*, London, Routledge & Kegan Paul, 1966.

37 Leonard, op. cit., p. 101.
38 Evans, op. cit.; R. Baker, 'Towards Generic Social Work Practice: A Review and Some Innovations', *British Journal of Social Work*, 5, 1975, pp. 193–215.
39 Pincus and Minahan, op. cit.
40 Goldstein, op. cit.
41 See C. Cockburn, *The Local State: Management of Cities and People*, London, Pluto Press, 1976, for an account of the importance of examining the impact of managerial and administrative requirements in the public definition of social problems.
42 See Bailey, op. cit., chapter 4, for a fuller description of the dangers of systems 'theory'.
43 J. Algie, *Social Values, Objectives and Action*, London, Kogan Page, 1975.
44 *Case Con*, issues since 1970; also see '*Case Con* Manifesto', in Bailey and Brake (eds), op.cit.
45 See M. Clarke, 'The Limits of Radical Social Work', *British Journal of Social Work*, 6, 1976, pp. 501–6; Cohen, op. cit.
46 T. Parsons, *The Social System*, New York, Free Press, 1951.
47 A. Gouldner, *The Coming Crisis of Western Sociology*, London, Heinemann, 1971, chapter 6.

Chapter 5 Planning and social theory

1 For a fuller exposition of this point see J. Bailey, *Social Theory for Planning*, London, Routledge & Kegan Paul, 1975.
2 For instance W. Ashworth, *The Genesis of Modern British Town Planning*, London, Routledge & Kegan Paul, 1954; G. Cherry, *The Evolution of British Town Planning*, London, Leonard Hill, 1974; G. Cherry, *Urban Change and Planning*, Henley, Foulis, 1972.
3 For an extension of this see G. Stedman Jones, 'History: the Poverty of Empiricism', in R. Blackburn (ed.), *Ideology in Social Science*, London, Fontana, 1972.
4 For instance J. Simmie, *Citizens in Conflict*, London, Hutchinson, 1974, chapter 2; R. Mellor, *Urban Sociology in an Urbanized Society*, London, Routledge & Kegan Paul, 1977, chapter 4.
5 For instance G. Cherry, *Town Planning in its Social Context*, London, Leonard Hill, 1970, p. 2.
6 For an analogous and more finely worked out description of liberalism in this sense see D. Harvey, *Social Justice and the City*, London, Arnold, 1973, pp. 147–52, in his discussion of 'status quo' and 'counter-revolutionary' theory.
7 The term is most famously used by Popper. K. Popper, *The Poverty of Historicism*, London, Routledge & Kegan Paul, 1957; examples are Simmie, op. cit., and L. Benevolo, *The Origins of Modern Town Planning*, London, Routledge & Kegan Paul, 1967.

8 The significance of this is embedded in the wider arguments about relative and absolute suffering. For an example of the effect of planning minimized see J. Westergaard and H. Resler, *Class in a Capitalist Society*, Harmondsworth, Penguin, 1976, pp. 133–4; Simmie, op. cit., chapter 5.

9 See Mellor, op. cit., pp. 144–5 for the structural conditions of this confidence. See J. B. McLoughlin, *Urban and Regional Planning : A Systems Approach*, London, Faber, 1969, pp. 19–57, for an example of its optimism.

10 See M. L. Harrison, 'British Town Planning Ideology and the Welfare State', *Journal of Social Policy*, 4, 1975, pp. 259–74.

11 Among those who note this are M. Kidron, *Western Capitalism Since the War*, London, Weidenfeld & Nicolson, 1968; J. K. Galbraith, *The New Industrial State*, Harmondsworth, Penguin, 1974; A. Shonfield, *Modern Capitalism*, London, Oxford University Press/RIA, 1965: a diverse group. Also, of course, it is typical of socialism as well; see J. Musil, 'The Development of Prague's Ecological Structure', in R. E. Pahl (ed.), *Readings in Urban Sociology*, Oxford, Pergamon, 1968; J. C. Fisher (ed.), *City and Regional Planning in Poland*, Ithaca, Cornell University Press, 1965.

12 A loose group of marxist and Marx-influenced writers including continental European historical materialists, Pahl, Harvey, Simmie and Mellor. See M. Harloe (ed.), *Captive Cities : Studies in the Political Economy of Cities and Regions*, New York, Wiley, 1977, introduction, for a sympathetic overview.

13 See any of the recent histories of academic sociology for the position and popularity of this subjectivism, for instance R. W. Friedrichs, *A Sociology of Sociology*, New York, Free Press, 1970.

14 A sophisticated version of this is L. Allison, *Environmental Planning*, London, Allen & Unwin, 1975.

15 For instance R. E. Pahl, *Whose City ?*, Harmondsworth, Penguin, 1975 (2nd edn).

16 For instance D. C. Foster, 'Planning and the Market', in P. Cowan (ed.), *The Future of Planning*, London, Heinemann, 1973.

17 Harvey, op. cit., pp. 276–8; also see D. Wedderburn, 'Facts and Theories of the Welfare State', in R. Miliband and J. Saville (eds), *Socialist Register 1965*, London, Merlin Press, 1965; J. Saville, 'The Welfare State: an Historical Approach', in E. Butterworth and R. Holman (eds), *Social Welfare in Modern Britain*, London, Fontana, 1975.

18 Simmie, op. cit., pp. 145–9.

19 See R. Miliband, *The State in Capitalist Society*, London Quartet, 1973.

20 See nearly all the contributors to C. G. Pickvance (ed.), *Urban Sociology : Critical Essays*, London, Tavistock, 1976.

21 N. Poulantzas, *Political Power and Social Classes*, London, New Left Books, 1971.

22 See I. Gough, 'State Expenditure in Advanced Capitalism', *New Left Review*, 92, 1975, pp. 53–92.

23 Pahl, 1975, op. cit. (published in the 1970 edition as chapter 14).

24 Ibid., chapter 13.

25 Notably P. Norman, 'Managerialism: A Review of Recent Work', in M.

Harloe (ed.), *Proceedings of the Conference on Urban Change and Conflict*, London, Centre for Environmental Studies, Conference Paper 14, 1975.

26 For instance N. Dennis, *People and Planning : The Sociology of Housing in Sunderland*, London, Faber, 1970; J. G. Davies, *The Evangelistic Bureaucrat*, London, Tavistock, 1972.

27 For instance Mellor, op. cit., p. 62. Her own argument, on p. 164, that relative autonomy can be seen in planners' influence over public housing design – business and financial interests not being directly affected – and that it has generally been to the detriment of the poor and inarticulate would seem more significant than she might allow, given that public housing accounts for more than one third of the total housing stock.

28 Dennis, op. cit. ; Davies, op. cit. ; N. Dennis, *Public Participation and Planners' Blight*, London, Faber, 1972; D. Muchnik, *Urban Renewal in Liverpool*, London, Bell, 1970; S. Damer, 'Wine Alley: The Sociology of a Dreadful Enclosure', *Sociological Review*, 22, 1974, pp. 221–42.

29 R. Goodman, *After the Planners*, Harmondsworth, Penguin, 1972, p. 53.

30 See chapter 2.

31 See E. Reade, 'Some educational consequences of the incorporation of the planning profession into the state bureaucracy', paper given at a conference of the Organisation of Sociologists in Polytechnics, Oxford Polytechnic, 1977, for a very general discussion of 'experts' and the 'corporate state'.

32 L. Peattie, 'Reflections on advocacy planning', *Journal of the American Institute of Planners*, 34, 1968, pp. 80–8.

33 See C. Cockburn, *The Local State : Management of Cities and People*, London, Pluto Press, 1976, chapter 4, for a critical account of 'the community approach'.

34 See J. McLoughlin, 'The Future of the Planning Profession', in Cowan (ed.), op. cit., and some of the 'professional' discussion, particularly *The Law Report : Planning and the Future*, London, Royal Town Planning Institute, 1976; J. Russell, 'Education Policy', *The Planner*, 63, 1977, pp. 148–9; P. Healey and M. Hebbert, 'Urban Governance: Some Comments on the RTPI discussion Paper "Planning and the Future" ', *Oxford Polytechnic Discussion Paper*, 1977.

35 For a discussion of a number of rationales for 'legitimacy', including technical expertise, see M. Rein, 'Social Planning: The Search for Legitimacy', *Journal of the American Institute of Planners*, 35, 1969, pp. 233–44.

36 A position argued fluently by D. Eversley, *The Planner in Society*, London, Faber, 1973.

37 For instance G. Benveniste, *The Politics of Expertise*, London, Croom Helm, 1973; D. Bell, *The Coming of Post-Industrial Society*, Harmondsworth, Penguin, 1974; and earlier by J. Meynaud, *Technocracy*, London, Faber, 1968.

38 For instance by T. Kitchen and J. Perry, 'Planning Education and Planning Research', *Journal of the Royal Town Planning Institute*, 57, 1971, pp. 455–7.

39 See Mellor, op. cit.; Cockburn, op. cit.; R. Hambleton, *Planning and Local Government*, London, Hutchinson, 1978.

40 See Bailey, op. cit., chapter 4.

41 For instance A. Faludi, *Planning Theory*, Oxford, Pergamon, 1973.

42 Noted by A. Ling, 'Planning – the next ten years', *Journal of the Royal Town Planning Institute*, 54, 1968, pp. 419–23.

43 In planning this is best seen in Goodman, op. cit.; C. A. Reich, *The Greening of America*, Harmondsworth, Penguin, 1971. For this kind of 'culture criticism' generally see H. Marcuse, *One-Dimensional Man*, London, Sphere, 1968; T. Roszak, *The Making of a Counter Culture*, London, Faber, 1970.

44 See Mellor, op. cit., pp. 156–66.

45 The thesis in Pahl, 1975, op. cit., does not eradicate the managerialist project, it locates it within a wider scheme of more profoundly independent variables.

46 Mellor, op. cit., p. 168.

47 See R. Williams, *The Country and the City*, London, Chatto & Windus, 1973.

48 As I tried to do in Bailey, op. cit., chapters 7 and 8, which contain extended discussion of the points made briefly below about European nineteenth-century theory and social ecology.

49 Especially M. Castells, 'Is there an urban sociology?', in Pickvance (ed.), op. cit.

50 Especially M. Weber, *The City*, Chicago, Free Press, 1958 (c. 1911); F. Tönnies, *Community and Society*, New York, Harper & Row, 1963 (1887). For a commentary see L. Reissman, *The Urban Process*, New York, Free Press, 1970, chapter VI; P. H. Mann, *An Approach to Urban Sociology*, London, Routledge & Kegan Paul, 1965, chapter 7; Mellor, op. cit., pp. 189–93.

51 See Reissman, op. cit., chapter V; Mellor, op. cit., chapter 6; G. A. Theodorson (ed.), *Studies in Human Ecology*, Evanston, Ill., Row, Peterson, 1963.

52 L. Wirth, 'Urbanism as a Way of Life', *American Journal of Sociology*, 44, 1938, pp. 1–24.

53 For an account of such 'levels' see C. G. A. Bryant, 'In defence of sociology: a reply to some contemporary philosophical criticisms', *British Journal of Sociology*, 21, 1975, pp. 95–107.

54 Pahl, 1975, op. cit., chapter 10.

55 See R. E. Pahl, 'Managers, Technical Experts and the State: Forms of Mediation, Manipulation and Dominance in Urban and Regional Development', in M. Harloe, 1977, op. cit.

56 Ibid., p. 53.

57 Pahl, 1975, op. cit.

58 See R. Pinker, *Social Theory and Social Policy*, London, Heinemann, 1971.

59 For a rare study of 'private' urban managers see J. Ford, 'The role of

building society managers in the urban stratification system: autonomy versus constraint', *Urban Studies*, 12, 1975, pp. 295–302; B. Elliott and D. McCrone, 'Landlords in Edinburgh: some preliminary findings', *Sociological Review*, 23, 1975, pp. 539–62.

60 See especially Pickvance (ed.), op. cit.; Harloe (ed.), *Captive Cities*; Pahl, 1975, op. cit.; Mellor, op. cit.

61 Including its 'own' journal, *The International Journal of Urban and Regional Research*.

62 M. Castells, *City, Class and Power*, London, Macmillan, 1978, is a recent collection of his work.

63 See especially L. Althusser, *For Marx*, London, Allen Lane, 1969; L. Althusser and E. Balibar, *Reading Capital*, London, New Left Books, 1970; N. Geras, 'Althusser's Marxism: an account and an assessment', *New Left Review*, 71, 1972, pp. 57–86.

64 See G. Therborn, *Science, Class and Society*, London, New Left Books, 1976, for a plain account.

65 In spite of attempts to minimize its relevance in Pickvance (ed.), op. cit., pp. 3–4; Harloe (ed.), 1977, op. cit., p. 3.

66 M. Castells, *The Urban Question*, London, Arnold, 1977.

67 Harloe (ed.), 1977, op. cit., introduction; and R. E. Pahl, 'Managers, Technical Experts and the State', in ibid.

68 A. W. Gouldner, 'The sociologist as partisan: sociology and the welfare state', *American Sociologist*, 3, 1968, pp. 103–16.

69 Harloe (ed.), 1975, op. cit., 'Position Paper', pp. 11.

70 Ibid., p. 1.

71 Ibid., and in Pickvance (ed.), op. cit.

72 Mellor, op. cit., p. 250.

73 C. G. Pickvance, 'From Social Base to Social Force: Some Analytical Issues in the Study of Urban Protest', in Harloe (ed.), 1977, op. cit.

74 Harloe (ed.), 1977, op. cit., p. 2.

75 Mellor, op. cit.; Pahl, 1977, op. cit.

76 See E. P. Thompson, *The Poverty of Theory and Other Essays*, London, Merlin Press, 1978, for trenchant criticisms.

77 R. Glass, 'Urban Sociology in Great Britain' (1955), in Pahl (ed.), 1968, op. cit.

78 R. Glass, 'Verbal Pollution' (review of M. Castells, *The Urban Question*, and M. Harloe (ed.), *Captive Cities*), *New Society*, 29 September 1977, pp. 667–9.

79 R. E. Pahl, '"Collective Consumption" and the State in Capitalist and State Socialist Societies', in R. Scase (ed.), *Industrial Society: Class, Cleavage and Control*, London, Allen & Unwin, 1977; 'Castells and Collective Consumption', *Sociology*, 12, 1978, pp. 309–15.

Chapter 6 Social theory for intervention

1 T. S. Kuhn, *The Structure of Scientific Revolutions*, Chicago, University of

Chicago Press, 1970 (2nd edn). Also see D. Crane, *Invisible Colleges*, University of Chicago Press, 1972; R. W. Friedrichs, *A Sociology of Sociology*, New York, Free Press, 1970.

2 For the USA see J. T. Carey, *Sociology and Public Affairs: The Chicago School*, London, Sage Foundation, 1975; L. L. Bernard and J. Bernard, *Origins of American Sociology*, New York, Crowell, 1943. For a self-consciously 'radical' view see H. and J. Schwendinger, *The Sociologists of the Chair*, New York, Basic Books, 1974. For Great Britain see P. Abrams, *The Origins of British Sociology, 1834–1914*, Harmondsworth, Penguin, 1968; R. J. Halliday, 'The Sociological Movement, the Sociological Society and the Genesis of Academic Sociology in Britain', *Sociological Review*, 26:3, vol. 16, 1968, p. 381.

3 For instance 'phenomenological sociology' or 'Althusserian historical materialism'.

4 See H. Marcuse, *One-Dimensional Man*, London, Sphere, 1968, p. 121.

5 See M. Castells and E. de Ipola, 'Epistemological Practice and the Social Sciences', *Economy and Society*, 5:2, 1976, pp. 111–44.

6 The most obvious British example is the work of the Centre for the Utilisation of Social Science Research at Loughborough University of Technology. See especially Monograph 1, 1972, 'Papers in Social Science Utilisation'.

7 This would be the thrust of Althusser's approach. See N. Geras, 'Althusser's Marxism: An Account and an Assessment', *New Left Review*, 71, 1972, pp. 57–86.

8 See D. Harvey, *Social Justice and the City*, London, Arnold, 1973, especially pp. 286–301, for an account of the relevance of the first two issue areas for any serious work.

9 See S. Cohen, 'It's Alright for you to Talk: Political and Sociological Manifestos for Social Action', in R. Bailey and M. Brake (eds), *Radical Social Work*, London, Arnold, 1975, p. 94.

10 J. Habermas, *Knowledge and Human Interests*, London, Heinemann, 1972, pp. 300–17; L. Goldman, *The Human Sciences and Philosophy*, London, Cape, 1969, Preface; G. Radnitzky, *Contemporary Schools of Metascience*, Göteborg, Akadamsförlaget, 1970 (2nd edn), vol. 2.

11 N. Rescher, *The Primary of Practice*, Oxford, Blackwell, 1973.

12 B. Fay, *Social Theory and Political Practice*, London, Allen & Unwin, 1975, especially note 5, p. 95.

13 Habermas, 1972, op. cit. pp. 314–17.

14 Or it involves at least one of Glucksmann's five kinds of theoretical work – epistemology, philosophy, substantive hypothesizing, methodology and description. M. Glucksmann, *Structuralist Analysis in Contemporary Social Thought*, London, Routledge & Kegan Paul, 1974.

15 See A. Wellmer, *Critical Theory of Society*, New York, Herder & Herder, 1971; R. Bernstein, *Praxis and Action*, London, Duckworth, 1972; A. Gouldner, *For Sociology*, Harmondsworth, Penguin, 1975, especially the essay 'The Two Marxisms'. Also see N. Lobkowicz, *Theory and Practice*.

Indiana, University of Notre Dame Press, 1967, for an excellent historical view of how mystification feeds on ambiguity in the meaning of this term.

16 L. Althusser, *For Marx*, London, Allen Lane, 1969; L. Althusser and E. Balibar, *Reading Capital*, London, New Left Books, 1970; L. Althusser, *Lenin and Philosophy and Other Essays*, London, New Left Books, 1971.

17 See Fay, op. cit., especially p. 95.

18 For instance Harvey, op. cit.

19 P. Abrams, op. cit.

20 See J. Madge, *The Tools of Social Science*, London, Longman, 1953; T. H. Marshall, *Sociology at the Crossroads*, London, Heinemann, 1963; T. S. Simey, *Social Science and Social Purpose*, London, Constable, 1968. It is worth remembering J. S. Mill's view that our own action and our evaluation of the actions of others are impossible without a prior theoretical base. J. S. Mill, 'On the Definition of Political Economy and on the Method of Scientific Investigation Proper to it' (1836), in E. Nagel (ed.), *J. S. Mill's Philosophy of Scientific Method*, New York, Hafner, 1950.

21 See C. W. Mills, *Sociology and Pragmatism*, New York, Galaxy, 1966.

22 Carey, op. cit.

23 See H. Lasswell, *A Pre-view of the Policy Sciences*, London, Elsevier, 1971; H. Orlans, *Contracting for Knowledge*, California, Jossey-Bass, 1973.

24 E.g. P. Halmos, 'The Moral Ambiguity of Critical Sociology', an otherwise very pertinent article in R. Fletcher (ed.), *The Science of Society and the Unity of Mankind*, London, Heinemann/BSA, 1974.

25 Misleadingly labelled variously 'positivism', 'empiricism', 'scientism', 'functionalism', and sometimes 'bourgeois ideology'. All straw men.

26 P. Filmer *et al.*, *New Directions in Sociological Theory*, London, Collier Macmillan, 1972; R. Turner (ed.), *Ethnomethodology*, Harmondsworth, Penguin, 1974.

27 M. Phillipson and M Roche, 'Phenomenology, Sociology and the Study of Deviance', in P. Rock and M. McIntosh (eds), *Deviance and Social Control*, London, Tavistock, 1974. This article is interesting in that it deals with a substantive object of sociology – rule making and breaking.

28 Ibid., pp. 151–3.

29 Habermas, op. cit., especially.

30 M. Jay, *The Dialectical Imagination*, London, Heinemann, 1974.

31 Marcuse, op. cit.

32 J. Habermas, 'Rationalism Divided in Two', in A. Giddens (ed.), *Positivism and Sociology*, London, Heinemann, 1974, pp. 219–21. See H. Albert, 'The Myth of Total Reason', in the same volume for a scathing attack on Habermas's mystification of 'dialectics' and 'hermeneutics'.

33 Wellmer, op. cit.

34 Albert, op. cit., p. 159.

35 Ibid.

36 Habermas, 1974, op. cit., p. 221.

37 W. Outhwaite, *Understanding Social Life: The Method called Verstehen*, London, Allen & Unwin, 1975, p. 16.

38 Horkheimer, quoted in Wellmer, op. cit., p. 16.

39 Althusser, 1969, 1970, 1971, ops. cit.

40 Especially in urban sociology: see C. G. Pickvance (ed.), *Urban Sociology: Critical Essays*, London, Tavistock, 1976: and M. Harloe (ed.), *Proceedings of the Conference on Urban Change and Conflict*, London, Centre for Environmental Studies, Conference Paper, 14, 1975.

41 See the exchange between Hindess and Pickvance in *Economy and Society*, 1973, following Hindess's article 'Models and Masks'.

42 Castells and de Ipola, op. cit.

43 See M. Glucksmann, op. cit., chapter 4.

44 See M. Castells, 'Theory and Ideology in Urban Sociology', in Pickvance (ed.), op. cit., pp. 75–80.

45 G. McDougall, J. Foulsham and J. Porter, 'Sociology in Planning: A Redefinition', paper read at Organisation of Sociologists in Polytechnics and Cognate Institutions Conference, 17.6.76, Lanchester Polytechnic.

46 See P. Q. Hirst, *Social Evolution and Sociological Categories*, London, Allen & Unwin, 1976.

47 The whole area of the 'sociology of knowledge' rests upon this issue and exemplifies a number of attempts to avoid or escape relativism. See P. Hamilton, *Knowledge and Social Structure*, London, Routledge & Kegan Paul, 1974.

48 Barrington Moore Jr, *Reflections on the Causes of Human Misery*, London, Allen Lane, 1972, and earlier, 'The Society Nobody Wants: A Look Beyond Marxism and Liberalism', in K. H. Wolff and B. Moore Jr (eds), *The Critical Spirit*, Boston, Beacon Press, 1967.

49 Ibid., pp. 5–12.

50 A. Tudor, 'Misunderstanding Everyday Life', *Sociological Review*, 24:3, 1976, pp. 505–18.

51 B. Bernstein, 'Sociology and the Sociology of Education: A Brief Account', in J. Rex (ed.), *Approaches to Sociology*, London, Routledge & Kegan Paul, 1974.

52 As must be obvious by this, this suggestion is rather like a version of Merton's 'middle range theory', but one in which analytic levels are specified in more than the purely formal terms which he uses. That is, whereas Merton is concerned with the generality of hypothesis levels (from grand to empirical propositions) I am suggesting a concern with levels of objects (albeit theoretical objects) of analysis.

53 R. Robertson, 'Towards the identification of the major axes of sociological analysis', in J. Rex (ed.), op. cit.

54 N. K. Denzin, *The Research Act in Sociology*, London, Butterworth, 1970.

55 A. Touraine, 'Towards a Sociology of Action', in Giddens, (ed.), op. cit.

56 T. B. Bottomore, *Sociology as Social Criticism*, London, Allen & Unwin, 1975, p. 49.

57 McDougall, Foulsham and Porter, op. cit.

58 R. Klima, 'Theoretical Pluralism, Methodological Dissension and the Role of the Sociologist: The West German Case', *Social Science Information*, II, 1972, pp. 69–108.

59 P. Feyerabend, 'Against Method: An Outline of an Anarchistic Theory of Knowledge', in M. Radner and S. Winokur (eds), *Minnesota Studies in the Philosophy of Science*, 4, Minneapolis, University of Minnesota Press, 1970.

60 I. Lakatos, 'The History of Science and its Rational Reconstructions', in R. Buck and R. Cohen (eds), *Boston Studies in the Philosophy of Science*, VIII, Dordrecht, Reidel, 1971.

61 R. K. Merton, 'Structural Analysis in Sociology', in P. Blau (ed.), *Approaches to the Study of Social Structure*, London, Open Books, 1976.

62 Merton, op. cit., p. 44

63 For instance A. W. Gouldner, *The Coming Crisis of Western Sociology*, London, Heinemann, 1971.

64 For a description of some of the basic 'unit ideas' of sociology see R. Nisbet, *The Sociological Tradition*, London, Heinemann, 1967.

65 See T. Benton, *Philosophical Foundations of the Three Sociologies*, London, Routledge & Kegan Paul, 1977, for the use of this term and an attempt to extend 'theoretical space'.

66 See C. G. A. Bryant, 'Kuhn, Paradigms and Sociology', *British Journal of Sociology*, 26, 1975, pp. 354–9, p. 357.

67 S. M. Eisenstadt and M. Curelaru, *The Form of Sociology: Paradigms and Crises*, New York, Wiley, 1976, p. 331.

68 For examples of such agendas see J. Habermas, *Knowledge and Human Interests*, London, Heinemann, 1972.

69 P. M. Worsley, 'The State of Theory and the Status of Theory', *Sociology*, 8, 1973, pp. 1–24, p. 4.

70 For this particular selection of criteria see N. Birnbaum, 'Sociology: Discontent Present and Perennial', *Social Research*, 38, 1973, pp. 732–50.

71 Gouldner, op. cit., chapter 2.

72 Respectively: P. Corrigan, 'Dichotomy is Contradiction: on "Society" as Constraint and Construction, Remarks on the Doctrine of the "Two Sociologies" ', *Sociological Review*, 23, 1975, pp. 221–44; Worsley, op. cit.; T. P. Wilson, 'Conceptions of Interaction and Forms of Explanation', *American Sociological Review*, 35, 1970, pp. 697–709; A. Dawe, 'The Two Sociologies', *British Journal of Sociology*, 21, 1970, pp. 207–18; P. Bandyopadhyay, 'Some Issues in Radical Sociology', *Sociological Review*, 19, 1971, pp. 5–29; L. H. Warshey, 'The Current State of Sociological Theory: Diversity, Polarity, Empiricism and Small Theories', *Sociological Quarterly*, 12, 1971, pp. 23–45.

73 The only writer on the list who even confronts the issue of dichotomy is Corrigan, op. cit.

74 Quoted by J. P. Gibbs, 'The Issue in Sociology', *Pacific Sociological Review*, 11, 1968, pp. 65–73.

75 T. S. Kuhn, *The Structure of Scientific Revolutions*, University of Chicago Press, 1962; Postscript 1969 to 2nd edn, 1970; 'Reflections on my Critics', in I. Lakatos and A. Musgrave (eds), *Criticism and the Growth of Knowledge*, Cambridge University Press, 1970.

76 For instance R. W. Friedrichs, *A Sociology of Sociology*, New York, Free Press, 1970.

77 See M. Masterman, 'The Nature of a Paradigm', in Lakatos and Musgrave (eds), op. cit.

78 See J. D. Urry, 'Thomas S. Kuhn as a Sociologist of Knowledge', *British Journal of Sociology*, 24, 1973, pp. 462–73; H. Martins, 'The Kuhnian "Revolution" and its Implications for Sociology', in J. J. Nossiter *et al.* (eds), *Imagination and Precision in the Social Sciences*, London, Faber, 1972; Bryant, op. cit.

79 A. Giddens, *New Rules of Sociological Method*, London, Hutchinson, 1976, p. 142. He mentions philosophers as widely spaced as Wittgenstein ('language games') and Althusser ('problematics').

80 Ibid., p. 144.

81 Eisenstadt and Curelaru, op. cit.

82 P. Halmos, *The Personal and the Political: Social Work and Political Action*, London, Hutchinson, 1978.

83 Ibid., p. 169.

Subject index

Ambiguity, 76, 128

Behavioural science, 14
Bureaucracy, 73

Capitalism, 101
Chicago school, 95–6
Classical urban sociology, 94–5
Community studies, 95
Conflict and consensus, 48–55
Conflict theories, 44, 64–5
Consensus theories, 44
Consumption, 83, 103, 112
Corporate state, 54
Criminology, 45–8; histories of, 46–7
Critical sociology, 110
Critical theory, 108
Criticism, 117
Culture, 78–9, 92–3, 104; autonomy
    of, 11–13; élite, 12–13; popular, 12

Deprofessionalization, 89
Dialectics, 110–11
Disciplines, 20, 24–32, 63, 105; basis
    of, 24–6; institutional conditions
    of, 26–8; objects of, 26; and
    planning, 91
Division of labour, 7, 23, 28, 29, 32;
    in professions, 63; in sociology, 72

Economics, 26, 33, 91
Empiricism, 102, 111–12
Ethical individualism, 55–7
Expert, 33

Frankfurt school, 110–11
Functionalism, 77–8

Hermeneutics, 110–11
Historical materialism, 98–103,
    111–13
Historicism, 81–3
History, liberal approach, 82–3
Humanities, 11–13

Idealism, 22
Individualism and collectivism, 55–9,
    69–70
Intellectuals, 34–6; autonomy, 22–3;
    humanist, 11–12; partisan, 34–6
Interventionism, 4, 50, 63, 105, 113,
    117, 118

Jurisprudence, 39–42; functions of,
    41–2; practical basis, 41; types of,
    40
Justice, 59

Knowledge, functions of, 23; pure,
    107–8; role in professions, 30–2

Law: analytic levels, 38;
    contributions of sociology, 41; and
    history, 42, 52, 53; and
    reductionism, 58; and social
    problems, 42–3; and sociology, 42;
    and sociology of knowledge, 41;
    theoretical underdevelopment, 40
Lawyers as professionals, 53–4
Legal change, 39
Legalism, 32
Legal knowledge, 39–42
Legal theory, 40–2

Market, 85–7

151

Name Index

153